Get Ready
for
Forever

Formerly: *Real Salvation*

R. A. Torrey

Publisher's Note

We rejoice to offer this classic collection of R. A. Torrey's fiery messages on heaven, hell, and salvation. The author's original language has been adapted to today's readership, but the anointing on Torrey's ministry is evident as he helps the reader face the question, "Where will I spend eternity?"

GET READY FOR FOREVER

R. A. Torrey

Edited by Diana L. Matisko

CONTENTS

Chapter 1

COME OUT OF HIDING

"Where art thou?"—Genesis 3:9.

The first question that God ever asked of man is recorded in Genesis 3:9, "Where art thou?" God asked the question of Adam on the evening of that awful day of the first sin. The voice of God in its majesty rolled down the avenues of the Garden of Eden. Until that day, the voice of God had been the sweetest music to Adam. He knew no greater joy than that of glad communion with his Creator and his heavenly Father. But now all was different. As the voice of God was heard in the Garden, Adam was filled with fear and tried to hide himself.

That is the history of every son of Adam from that day until now. Every sinner is trying to hide from the presence and the all-seeing eye of God. That accounts for a large share of the scepticism, agnosticism, and atheism of our day. It is sinful man trying to hide from a holy God.

True Reasons For Unbelief

Men will give you many reasons why they are sceptics, agnostics, or atheists. But in the majority of cases, the real reason is this—sinful men hope to hide themselves from the discomfort of God's presence by denying that He exists. That also accounts for much of the neglect of the Bible. People will tell you that they do not read their Bibles because they have so much else to read or because they are not interested in the Bible. They declare that it is a dull and stupid book to them. But the true cause of man's neglect of Bible study is this: the Bible brings God near to us as no other book does, and men are uneasy when they become conscious of the presence of God. Therefore, they neglect the book that brings God near.

This also accounts for much of the absenteeism from the house of God and its services. People will give you many reasons why they do not attend church. They will tell you they cannot dress well enough to attend church or that they are too busy and too tired. They will complain that the services are dull and uninteresting. But the reason why men and women, old and young, are habitually absent from church is because the house of God brings God near and makes them uncomfortable in sin.

No man ever succeeded in hiding from God. God said to Adam, "Where art thou?" Adam had to come from his hiding place to meet God face to face and make full confession of his sin. Sooner or later, no matter how carefully we hide ourselves from God, every man and woman will have to come from their hiding place and meet Him face to face. They will have to make a full declaration of exactly where they stand in His presence.

God puts the question of the text to every Christian and to everyone who is not a Christian. "Where art thou?" Where do you stand concerning spiritual and eternal things? Where do you stand concerning God, heaven, righteousness, Christ, and eternity? "Where art thou?"

Knowing Where You Stand

Every truly intelligent person desires to know just where he is. Every wise businessman desires to know where he stands financially. In our country, every careful businessman periodically takes an inventory of his stock, examines his accounts, finds out precisely what are his credits and debits, and how much his assets exceed or fall below his liabilities.

He may discover as a result of his scrutiny that he does not stand as well as he thought he did. If that is true, he wants to know it in order that he may conduct his business accordingly. Many have failed in business through unwillingness to face facts and find out just where they stood.

I knew a very brilliant businessman who was truly gifted in a certain type of business enterprise. But his affairs got into a tangled condition.

His wise business friends came to him and advised him to go through his books and find out just where he stood. They said to him, "If you are in bad shape, we will help you out."

But the man was too proud to take their advice. He was too proud to admit that his business was in danger of failure, so he refused to look into it. He resolutely tried to plunge through. But instead of plunging through, he plunged into utter financial ruin. Although he was an exceptionally brilliant man in some areas, he experienced complete financial shipwreck. He never got on his feet again. When he died he did not have enough money to pay his funeral expenses, simply because he was not willing to humble his pride and face facts.

Many people are too proud to face the fact that they are morally and spiritually bankrupt. So they are going to grit their teeth and plunge through. They will plunge into utter and eternal ruin.

Every man wants to know where he stands physically. He wants to know the condition of his lungs, heart, stomach, and nerves. He may be worse off than he thinks he is. He may think his heart is sound when it is defective. But he wants to know it, because then he will not subject it to the strain that he otherwise would. Many lie in a premature grave who might be doing good work on earth because they were not willing to find out what their real condition was and act accordingly.

Every man at sea wishes to know where his vessel is, its exact latitude and longitude. When crossing the Atlantic Ocean some years ago, we sailed for days beneath clouds and through fogs. We were unable to take an observation by the sun and had been sailing blindly. One night I happened to be on deck, when suddenly there was a rift in the clouds, and the North Star appeared. Word was sent below, and the captain of the vessel hurried on deck. I remember how he nearly laid across the compass as he carefully took an observation by the North Star, that he might know exactly where we were.

We are all sailing across a perilous sea toward an eternal port. Every truly intelligent man and woman will desire to know just where they are— their exact spiritual longitude and their exact spiritual latitude.

How To Evaluate The Question

Let us consider this weighty question of where we are. We should consider it *seriously*. It is not a question to trifle with. It is amazing that men and women may be sensible about everything else and would not think of trifling with the great financial questions of the day or with great social problems. But they treat this great question of eternity as a joke.

One evening I bought a paper from a little newsboy on the street. As he handed me my change, I asked him, "My boy, are you saved?" The boy treated it as a joke. I was not surprised. That is all

9

you would expect of a poor, uneducated newsboy on the street. But it is not what you would expect of thinking men and women when you come to these great eternal problems of God, eternity, salvation, heaven, and hell.

Anyone who trifles with questions like these is a fool. I don't care about your culture, your social position, or your reputation. Unless you face the great question of your spiritual condition with the most profound earnestness and seriousness, you are playing the part of a fool.

We should consider this question *honestly*. Many people today try to deceive themselves, others, and even God. They know in their innermost hearts that they are wrong, but they try to persuade themselves, others, and God that they are right.

You cannot deceive God. It will do you no good to deceive anybody else, and it is the height of folly to deceive yourself. The biggest fool on earth is the man who fools himself. Be honest. If you are lost, admit it; if you are on the road to hell, acknowledge it; if you are not a Christian, say so. If you are an enemy of God, face the facts. If you are a child of the devil, realize it. Be honest with yourself, honest with your fellowmen, and honest with God.

We should consider the question *thoroughly*. Many people are honest and serious to a certain point, but they don't go to the bottom of things. They are superficial. They give these tremendous questions a few moments' thought, and then their weak minds grow weary. They say, "I guess I am all right; I will take my chances."

No one can afford to guess on questions like these. We must be absolutely certain. It will not satisfy me to hope I am saved; I must know that I am saved. It will not satisfy me to hope I am a child of God; I must know that I am a child of God. It will not satisfy me to hope that I am bound for heaven; I must know that I am bound for heaven. Do not lay these questions down until you have gone to the bottom of them and know for certain just where you stand.

We should consider these questions *prayerfully*. God tells us in His Word, and we know from experience, that the heart is deceitful above all things and desperately wicked. (See Jeremiah 17:9.) There is nothing that the human heart is as deceitful about as our moral and spiritual condition. Every man and woman is by nature sharp-sighted to the faults of others and blind to their own faults. We need to face this question in prayer. You will never know where you stand until God shows you.

We must pray like David, "Search me, O God, and know my heart: try me, and know my thoughts: And see if there be any wicked way in me" (Psalm 139:23-24). Only when God sheds the light of His Holy Spirit into our hearts and shows us ourselves as *He* sees us will we ever know ourselves as we truly are. To see ourselves in

11

the light of God's presence, as God sees us, will only be in answer to definite and earnest prayer.

Are You A Religious Person?

One morning I met the minister of a church which I formerly pastored. He said to me, "Brother Torrey, I had an awful experience this morning."

I said, "What was it, Brother Norris?"

He mentioned a member of the church. "You know she is dying. She sent for me to come and see her this morning. I hurried to her home. The moment I opened the door and entered the room she cried from her bed, 'Oh, Brother Norris, I have been a professing Christian for forty years. I am now dying and have just found out that I was never saved at all.' "

The horror of it! To be a professing Christian for forty years and never find out until your life is at an end that you have never really been a Christian at all. It is better to find it out today than in eternity.

Many men and women have been professing Christians for years but were never saved. In a paper edited by a clergyman, I read a letter complaining about our meetings. The writer said, "These men produced the impression that some of our church members are not saved." Well, that is the impression we tried to produce, for that is the truth of God. In churches throughout the world, you will find many men and women who are unsaved.

Once more we should consider this question scripturally, according to the Book. God has given to you and me only one safe chart and compass to guide us on our voyage through life toward eternity. That chart and compass is the Bible. If you steer your course according to the Book, you will steer safely. If you steer according to your own feelings, according to the speculation of the petty philosopher or the theologian, according to anything but the clear declaration of the Word of God, you steer your course to shipwreck. Any hope that is not founded on the clear, unmistakable teaching of God's Word is absolutely worthless.

You Can Be Sure

In one of my pastorates, a young married couple had a sweet little child entrusted to them by the heavenly Father. Then one day, that little child went home to be with the Lord. In the hour of their sorrow, I went to call upon the grieving parents. Taking advantage of their tenderness of heart, I pointed them to the Savior with whom their child was safely at home. They promised to accept Jesus as their Savior.

After some days and weeks had passed and the first shock of the sorrow had gone, they began to drift back into the world again. I called upon them to speak with them. Only the wife was at home. I began by talking about the little child and how safe and happy he was in the arms of Jesus. To all of this she gladly assented. Then I turned the topic a little bit and said to her, "Do you expect to see your child again?"

"Oh," she said, "certainly. I have no doubt that I will see my child again."

I said, "Why do you expect to see your child again?"

"Because the child is with Jesus, and I expect when I die I shall go to be with Him, too."

I said, "Do you think you are saved?"

"Oh, yes," she replied, "I think I am saved."

"Why do you think you are saved?"

"Because I feel so," she said.

"Is that your only ground of hope?"

"That is all."

I said, "Your hope is not worth anything."

That seemed cruel, didn't it? But it was kind. I asked her, "Can you put your finger upon anything in the Word of God that proves you have everlasting life?"

"No," she said, "I cannot."

"Well, then," I said, "your hope is absolutely worthless."

Then she turned on me, which she had a perfect right to do. It is quite right to talk back to preachers—I believe in it—and she began to talk back.

"Do you expect to go to heaven when you die?"

I said, "Yes, I know I shall."

14

"When you die, do you expect to be with Christ?"

"Yes," I said, "I know I shall."

"Do you think you have everlasting life?"

"Yes," I said, "I know I have."

"Can you put your finger on anything in the Word of God that proves you have eternal life?"

I said, "Yes, thank God, John 3:36, 'He that believeth on the Son hath everlasting life.' I know I believe on the Son of God. On the sure ground of God's Word, I know I have everlasting life."

Chapter 2

WHERE DO YOU STAND?

"Choose you this day whom ye will serve"—
Joshua 24:15.

A few suggestions will help you in considering the question, "Where art thou?" *Are you saved or are you lost?* You are one or the other. Unless you have been definitely saved by a definite acceptance of Jesus Christ, you are definitely lost. Only two classes exist—lost sinners and saved sinners. To which class do you belong?

Are you on the road to heaven or the road to hell? You are on one or the other. The Lord Jesus tells us that there are only two roads—the broad road that leads to destruction and the narrow road that leads to life everlasting. (See Matthew 7:13-14.) Which road are you on? Are you on the road that leads to God and heaven and glory? Or are you on the road that leads down to Satan, sin, shame, and hell?

Some years ago, an English sailor came into a mission in New York City. As he left the mission not very much affected, a worker at the door put a little card into his hand. On this card these words were printed: "If I should die tonight I would go to_____." The place was left blank, and underneath was written, "Please fill in and sign your name."

The sailor, without even reading the card, put it in his pocket and went down to the steamer. In the journey back to England, he was thrown from the rigging and broke his leg. They took him down to his berth, and as he lay there day after day, that card stared him in the face. "If I should die tonight I would go to_____."

"Well," he said, "if I filled that out honestly, I would have to write—*hell*. If I would die tonight, I would go to hell. But I won't fill it out that way." Lying there in his berth, he accepted Jesus Christ as his Lord and Savior and filled out the card—"If I would die tonight, I would go to heaven." One day he went back to New York. He walked into the mission and handed in the card with his name signed to it.

Suppose you had such a card to complete. "If I would die tonight, I would go to_____." What would it be?

Are you a child of God or a child of the devil?
We live in a day in which many superficial thinkers are telling us that all men are the children of God. That is not the teaching of the Bible, and it is not the teaching of Jesus Christ. Jesus Christ says distinctly in John 8:44, talking to certain Jews,

17

"Ye are of your father the devil." We are told in 1 John 3:10, "In this the children of God are manifest, and the children of the devil." And we are told distinctly in John 1:12, "As many as received him, to them gave he power to become the sons of God." Every one of us is either a child of God or a child of the devil. Which are you?

When I was speaking in the city of Ballarat in Australia, there sat a long line of educated men listening to the sermon. I was preaching on the difference between the children of God and the children of the devil. The next night when I gave the invitation, almost the entire line of educated men came to the front. When they got up to give their testimony, one of them said, "The reason why I came tonight and accepted Christ was this: I was here last night and heard Dr. Torrey say that everyone was a child of God or a child of the devil. I knew I was not a child of God; therefore, I knew I must be a child of the devil. I made up my mind I would be a child of the devil no longer. I have come forward tonight to take Jesus Christ."

Are you a mere formal Christian or a real Christian? You know there are two kinds. Are you one of these men or women who call themselves Christians, who go to the house of God on Sunday, take communion, or perhaps teach a Bible class or a Sunday school class? But the rest of the week, do you run around drinking, carousing, and participating in all the frivolity and foolishness of the world?

Are you one of these Christians who are trying to hold on to Jesus Christ with the one hand and to the world with the other? Or are you a real Christian who has renounced the world with your whole heart and given yourself to Jesus Christ, a Christian who can sing and mean it, "I surrender all"? "Where art thou?" What kind of a Christian are you?

Are you for Christ or against Him? You are either one or the other. We read in Matthew 12:30, in the words of Jesus Himself, "He that is not with me is against me." Either you are with Jesus wholeheartedly and openly, or else you are against Jesus. Which are you? For Christ or against Him?

Taking A Stand

In my first pastorate, year after year, there came an outpouring of God's Spirit. In one of these gracious outpourings, a great many of the leading businessmen of the area were converted. It was a small town, but one of the businessmen would not take a stand. He was one of the most exemplary men in the community. He was an amiable, upright, regular attender at church. He was a member of my Bible class and the choir. But he was one of those men who wanted to please both sides. He was identified with friends in business, in community action groups, and elsewhere, who were not committed Christians. He was afraid that

19

he would offend them if he came out boldly and honestly for Christ.

The weeks passed by. One Sunday morning, he was leaving my Bible class and passed by the superintendent of the Sunday school, who was his intimate friend. They had been in the army together. As he passed by, his friend turned to him and said, "George?"

"Well, what is it, Porter?" said the other, calling him by his first name.

"George, when are you going to take a stand?"

He said, "Ring the bell."

Promptly the superintendent stepped up to the bell and rang it. The congregation turned in surprise, wondering what was going to happen. George stepped to the front of the platform. It was a community where everybody knew everybody else by their first name, and everybody was curious.

"Friends," he said, "I have heard it said time and time again during these meetings that a man must either be for Jesus Christ or against Him. I want you all to know that from this time on, my wife and I are for Christ."

There are many people who have been involved in a church for years, but they have never taken an open stand for Christ. Take it now. Say, "As for me and my house, we are for Christ."

It is important to face the question, "Where art thou?" Where you are today may determine where you will spend eternity.

Meeting The Chief Physician

A story is told of Dr. Forbes Winslow, an eminent pathologist in diseases of the mind. A young French nobleman came to London bringing letters of introduction from leading Frenchmen. The letters introduced him to Dr. Forbes Winslow and requested the doctor's best care for the young man. He presented his letters, and Dr. Winslow said, "What is your trouble?"

"Dr. Winslow, I cannot sleep. I have not had a good night's sleep for two years. Unless something is done for me, I will go insane."

Dr. Winslow said, "Why can't you sleep?"

"Well," said the young man, "I can't tell you."

Dr. Winslow said, "Have you lost any money?"

"No," he said, "I have lost no money."

"Have you lost friends?"

"No, I have lost no friends recently."

"Have you suffered in honor or reputation?"

"Not that I know of."

"Well then," said the doctor, "why can't you sleep?"

The young man said, "I would rather not tell you."

"Well," said Dr. Winslow, "if you don't tell me, I can't help you."

"Well," he said, "if I must tell you, I will. I am an agnostic. My father was an agnostic before me. Every night when I lie down to sleep, I am confronted with the question, 'Eternity—where shall

I spend it?' All night that question rings in my ears. If I succeed in getting off to sleep, my dreams are worse than my waking hours, and I awaken again."

Dr. Winslow said, "I can't do anything for you."

"What!" said the young Frenchman. "Have I come all the way over here from Paris for you to help me, and you dash my hopes to the ground? Do you mean to tell me that my case is hopeless?"

Dr. Winslow repeated, "I can do nothing for you, but I can tell you about a Physician who can." He walked across his study, took up his Bible from the center of the table, and opened it to Isaiah 53:5-6. He began to read: "He was wounded for our trangressions, he was bruised for our iniquities: the chastisement of our peace was upon him; and with his stripes we are healed. All we like sheep have gone astray; we have turned every one to his own way; and the Lord hath laid on him the iniquity of us all."

Looking at the Frenchman, he said, "That is the only Physician in the world that can help you."

There was a curl of scorn upon the Frenchman's lip. He said, "Dr. Winslow, do you mean to tell me that you, an eminent scientist, believe in that worn-out superstition of the Bible and Christianity?"

"Yes," said Dr. Winslow. "I believe in the Bible. I believe in Jesus Christ. And believing in the Bible and believing in Jesus Christ has saved me from becoming what you are today."

The young fellow thought for a moment. Then

he said, "Dr. Winslow, if I am an honest man, I should at least be willing to consider it, correct?"

"Yes, sir."

"Well," he said, "will you explain it to me?"

The eminent physician sat down with his open Bible, and for several days, he showed the young Frenchman the way of eternal life. He saw Christ as his divine, atoning Savior, put his trust in Him, and went back to Paris with peace of mind. He had solved the great question of eternity and where he would spend it, for he would spend it with Christ in glory.

Eternity—where will you spend it?

Chapter 3

WHY DO YOU NOT BELIEVE?

"He that believeth not is condemned already, because he hath not believed in the name of the only begotten Son of God"—John 3:18.

The failure to put faith in Jesus Christ is not a mere misfortune. It is a sin—a grievous sin, an appalling sin, a damning sin. Men will tell you very lightly, as if it were something of which they were quite proud, "I do not believe in Jesus Christ." Few men are foolish, blind, or utterly depraved enough to tell you proudly, "I am a murderer," or "I am an adulterer," or "I am a habitual liar." Yet, none of these are a sadder or darker confession than, "I am an unbeliever in Jesus Christ."

Believing or not believing in Jesus Christ is largely a matter of the will. Some people imagine it is wholly a matter of intellectual conviction. The one who assumes this is a very superficial thinker. There are few people who do not have sufficient evidence that Jesus is the Son of God and the Savior of those who believe in Him. They must only be willing to yield themselves to the evidence.

Men and women who believe on Jesus Christ have decided to yield to the truth. They believe on Him who is clearly proven to be God's Son. Those who do not believe because of the love of sin, or for some other reason, will not yield to the truth and accept Him as Savior and Lord.

Your refusal to accept Jesus Christ is not because you have honest reasons for believing that He is not what He claims to be. You know it is because you do not want to accept Him and surrender your life to Him. This is a great sin—greater than any sin you can commit against any person by lying to him, stealing from him, or killing him.

Facing The Truth

Don't try to ignore the truth. If you do, you will do it to your eternal ruin. If I am right in this matter, and if the Bible is right, it is infinitely important that you know it. Therefore, read carefully and be honest with yourself.

Unbelief in Jesus Christ is an appalling sin because of the dignity of the person Jesus Christ. Jesus is the Son of God in a sense that no other person is the Son of God. "Who being the brightness of his glory, and the express image of his person" (Hebrews 1:3).

"In him dwelleth all the fullness of the Godhead bodily" (Colossians 2:9). "When he bringeth in the firstbegotten into the world, he saith, And let all the angels of God worship him" (Hebrews 1:6). "That all men should honour the Son, even as they honour the Father" (John 5:23).

A dignity belongs to Jesus Christ that belongs to no angel or archangel and to none of the principalities or powers in the heavenly places. His is the name that is above every name, that at the name of Jesus every knee should bow and every tongue confess that Jesus Christ is Lord. (See Philippians 2:10.)

An injury done to Jesus Christ is a sin of vastly greater magnitude than a sin done to man. A mule has rights, but its rights are unimportant when compared to the rights of a man. The law recognizes the rights of a mule, but the killing of a mule is not regarded as serious as the putting out of a man's eye. But the rights of a man, even of the purest, noblest, greatest of men, pale into insignificance before the rights of the infinite God and His infinite Son, Jesus Christ.

God's Majesty And Our Sin

To realize the enormity of a sin committed against Jesus Christ, we must strive for an adequate conception of His dignity and majesty. When we do, we see that our unbelief robs this infinitely glorious Person of the honor due Him.

What was it that struck conviction into the hearts of three thousand men on the day of Pentecost and made them cry out in agony, "Men and brethren, what shall we do?" (Acts 2:37). It was this—Peter, filled with the Spirit, told them who Jesus was. He said, "Therefore let all the house of Israel know assuredly, that God hath made that same Jesus, whom ye have crucified, both Lord and Christ" (Acts 2:36). Their eyes were opened at last to see the glory, dignity, and majesty of the Person they had so outrageously wronged. All the sins of their lifetime instantly seemed to be nothing in comparison with this sin.

If you permit God to open your eyes to see who Jesus is, to see His infinite dignity, glory, and majesty, you will see that every wrong done to any mere man is nothing compared to the wrong done to this holy and majestic Person. You may refuse to let God open your eyes to the infinte glory of Jesus. You may say, "I don't see that He is essentially greater than other men or that His rights are more sacred than those of Longfellow, Lincoln, Washington, or my next-door neighbor. But the day will come when you will have to see.

The full glory of Jesus will be unveiled to the whole universe. If you will not repent now and receive pardon for your awful sin of unbelief, you will be overwhelmed with eternal shame. You will cry for the rocks and the hills to fall upon you and hide you from the wrath of Him who sits upon the throne of the universe. (See Revelation 6:15-17.) You will wish to run from the presence of glory into eternal darkness if only you could escape the presence of Him whom you have so grievously wronged. On and on you would wish to flee from the outraged Son of God.

One night God gave me a vision of the glory of Jesus Christ. I saw the appalling nature of sin against Him, this infinitely glorious One. You may not have had such a vision, and you do not need to have it. You know what God's testimony regarding Jesus is. That testimony is in His Word. In that testimony, you will find that the most grievous wrong against man—theft, adultery, murder—is as nothing. For this reason our text says, "He that believeth on him is not condemned: but he that believeth not is condemned already, because he hath not believed in the name of the only begotten Son of God" (John 3:18).

Unbelief in Jesus Christ is an appalling sin because faith is the supreme thing He is entitled to receive. Jesus is worthy of many things. He is worthy of our admiration, our attention, our obedience, our service, and our love—all these things are His due. Not to give Him these things is to rob a Being of infinite importance of what is rightly His.

Above all else, Jesus Christ is worthy of faith. Man's confidence belongs in Jesus Christ. He is infinitely worthy of the surrender of our intellects, our feelings, and our wills. It is right for you to go to Him and say, "Lord Jesus, infinite Son of God, I surrender to You my faith, the confidence of my heart, and my will." If you refuse to do that, you have robbed Jesus Christ. You have robbed this glorious, divine Person of His first and greatest right, robbed a divine Person of His supreme due. So it is written in our text, "He that believeth not is condemned already, because he hath not believed in the name of the only begotten Son of God."

Unbelief in Jesus Christ is an appalling sin because He is the incarnation of all the infinite moral perfections of God's own being. "God is light, and in him is no darkness at all" (1 John 1:5). This infinite, absolute light and this infinite holiness, love, and truth is incarnate in Jesus Christ. The refusal to accept Him is the refusal of light and the choice of darkness. The one who rejects Him loves darkness rather than light. Nothing more clearly reveals a man's heart than what he chooses and what he rejects. A man who chooses dirty books, indecent pictures, and worldly friends is a foul man despite what he pretends to be. A man who rejects the good, the pure, and the true is bad, impure, and false. To reject Christ is to reject the infinite light of God. It reveals a corrupt heart that loves darkness rather than light.

It is written in our text, "He that believeth not is condemned already, because he hath not believed in the name of the only begotten Son of God. And this is the condemnation, that light is come into the world, and men loved darkness rather than light, because their deeds were evil" (John 3:18-19).

Unbelief in Jesus Christ is an appalling sin because it is trampling underfoot the infinite love and mercy of God. Jesus Christ is the supreme expression of God's love and mercy to sinners. "For God so loved the world, that he gave his only begotten Son, that whosoever believeth in him should not perish, but have everlasting life" (John 3:16).

We have all broken God's holy laws and brought the wrath of the Holy One upon ourselves. But God still loves us. Instead of banishing us forever from His presence into the darkness where there is only agony and despair, He provided salvation for us at infinite cost to Himself. His saving love had no limit, and it stopped at no sacrifice. He gave His best—His only begotten Son—to redeem us. All that we need to do to be saved is to believe on that Son and put our trust in the pardoning mercy and love of God.

But instead of believing and obtaining eternal life, what are you doing? You are not believing; you are rejecting the love and its provision. You are despising and trampling underfoot the salvation which God purchased with the blood of His Son and offered to you. Unbelief in Jesus Christ scorns and insults infinite pardoning love. Every man or woman, young and old, who does not place the faith of their whole being in Jesus Christ and receive Him as their Lord and Savior is guilty of scorning and insulting the infinite, pardoning love of God.

Some even go beyond that. They try to make themselves believe that Jesus is not the Son of God and that there is no need of an atonement. They laugh at the sacrifice the loving Father has made in order that His guilty, hell-deserving subjects might be saved. One sometimes wonders why the love of God does not turn to blazing wrath and why God does not blast the world of Christ-rejecting men with the breath of His mouth.

There are other reasons why unbelief in Jesus Christ is an appalling sin, but these four tremendous reasons are enough:

1. Because of the infinite dignity of His person.

2. Because faith is rightly His, and withholding it robs a divine Person of His supreme due.

3. Because Jesus Christ is the incarnation of all the infinite moral perfection of God's own being.

4. Because it tramples underfoot the infinite love and mercy of God.

Unbelief in Jesus Christ is an appalling sin. Theft is a gross sin; adultery is worse; and murder is shocking. But all these are nothing compared to the violation of the dignity and majesty of Jesus Christ, the only begotten Son of God, by our unbelief. How God must abhor the sin of unbelief! How all holy men and women must despise the sin of unbelief!

Not only the agnostic and the sceptic are guilty of this sin, but everyone who holds back from the wholehearted surrender of his mind, affections, and will. All who fail to gladly welcome Jesus as Savior and Lord are guilty of this appalling sin. Do you cry out as the three thousand at Pentecost did, "What shall we do?" Soften your heart of stone, publicly confess your awful sin, and forsake it forever. Don't rest another day under such awful guilt.

We see why unbelief leads to eternal doom. No matter how many good things a man may do, he must forever perish if he refuses to believe in Jesus Christ. Give up your unbelief in Jesus Christ and receive Him now.

Chapter 4

THE REALITY OF HELL

"And if thy right eye offend thee, pluck it out, and cast it from thee: for it is profitable for thee that one of thy members should perish, and not that thy whole body should be cast into hell"— Matthew 5:29.

If I were able to choose my own subject to write about, I certainly would never choose hell. It is an awful subject, but a minister of God has no right to choose his own subjects. He must go to God for them and faithfully teach what God has commanded.

I wish that I could believe that there was no hell. That is, I wish that I could believe that all men would repent and accept Christ, and that hell would therefore be unnecessary. Of course, if men persist in sin and persist in the rejection of Christ, it is right that there should be a hell.

If men choose sin, it is for the good of the universe and the glory of God that there is a hell to confine them in. But I wish with all my heart that all men would repent and render hell unnecessary. But I cannot believe it if it is not true. I would rather believe unpleasant truth than to believe pleasant error. As awful as the thought is, I have been driven to the conclusion that there is a hell.

I once honestly believed and taught that all men, and even the devil, would ultimately come to repentance, and that hell would one day cease to be. But I could not honestly reconcile this position with the teaching of Christ and the apostles. I finally decided that I must either give up my Bible or give up my eternal hope.

I could not give up the Bible. I had become thoroughly convinced that the Bible, beyond a doubt, was the Word of God. I could not twist and distort the Scriptures to make them agree with what I wanted to believe. As an honest man, there was only one thing left for me to do—give up my opinion that all men would ultimately come to repentance and be saved.

The Painful Truth

I know that if a man stands squarely upon the teaching of Christ and the apostles and declares it without fear, he will be called "narrow," "harsh," and "cruel." But I have no desire to be any more broad than Jesus Christ was. Is it cruel to tell men the truth? The kindest thing that one can do is to declare the whole counsel of God and show men the full measure of their danger.

Suppose I was walking down a railroad track, knowing that far behind me there was a train coming on loaded with happy travelers. I come to a place where I had supposed that there was a bridge across the chasm. But to my horror, I find that the bridge is down. I say to myself, "I must go back at once as far as possible up the track and stop that oncoming train."

My awful warning that the bridge is down and that the passengers are in peril of a frightful disaster spoils the merriment of the evening. Would that be cruel? Would it not be the kindest thing that I could do?

Suppose when I found the bridge down, I had said, "These people are so happy. I cannot bear to disturb their light-heartedness and pleasure. That would be too cruel. I will sit down here and wait until the train comes." Then I sit down while the train comes rushing on and leaps unwarned into that awful abyss. Soon I would hear the despairing shrieks and groans of the wounded and mangled as they crawl out from among the corpses of the dead. Would that be kind? Would it not be the cruelest thing that I could do? If I acted that way, I would be arrested for manslaughter.

I have been down the track. I thought that there was a bridge across the chasm, but I have found that the bridge is down. Many of you who are now full of laughter are rushing on unwarned of the awful fate that awaits you. I have come back up the track to warn you. I may destroy your present merriment, but by God's grace I will save you from the awful doom. Is that cruel?

I would much rather be called cruel for being kind, than be called kind for being cruel. The cruelest man on earth is the man who believes the stern things we are told in the Word of God about the future penalties of sin but avoids declaring them because they are unpopular.

The Danger Of Man's Philosophies

I will not give you my own speculations about the future destiny of those who refuse to repent. Man's speculations on such a subject are absolutely worthless. God knows; we don't. But God has told us much of what He knows about it. Let us listen to Him. One ounce of God's revelation about the future is worth a hundred tons of man's speculation. What difference does it make what you or I think? The question is: What does God say?

"And if thy right eye offend thee, pluck it out, and cast it from thee: for it is profitable for thee that one of thy members should perish, and not that thy whole body be cast into hell" (Matthew 5:29).

It is absolutely certain that there is a hell. There are people who will tell you that all the scholarly ministers and clergymen have given up belief in hell. That simply is not so. That kind of argument is a favorite with men who know that they have a weak case. They try to bolster it up by strong assertions.

It is true that some scholarly ministers have given up belief in hell, but they never gave it up for reasons of Greek or New Testament scholarship. They gave it up for purely sentimental and speculative reasons. If a man goes to the New Testament to find out the truth and not to see how he can twist it into conformity with his speculations, he will find hell in the New Testament.

But suppose that every scholarly minister had given up belief in hell. It would not prove anything. Everybody that is familiar with the history of the world and the history of the Church knows that time and time again the scholars have all given up belief in doctrines that in the final outcome proved to be true.

There were no scholars in Noah's day who believed there would be a flood. But the flood came just the same. There were no scholars in Lot's day who believed that God would destroy Sodom and Gomorrah, but He did. Jeremiah and one friend were the only leading men in all Jerusalem who believed what Jeremiah taught about the coming destruction of Jerusalem under Nebuchadnezzar. But history outside the Bible, as well as history in the Bible, tells us that it came true to the very letter.

Every leading school of theological thought in the days of Jesus Christ—the Pharisees, the Sadducees, the Herodians, and the Essenes—every one of the four scoffed at Jesus Christ's prediction about the coming judgment of God upon Jerusalem. But secular history tells us that, in spite of the dissent of all the scholars, it came true just as Jesus predicted.

There was scarcely a leading scholar in the days of Luther and Huss that had not given up faith in the doctrine of justification by faith. Luther, and their colleagues had to establish a new university to stand for the truth of God. But today we know that Martin Luther was right, and every university of Germany, France, England, and Scotland was wrong. So, if it were true that every scholarly preacher on earth had given up belief in the doctrine of hell, it would not prove anything.

What The Bible Says

Hell is certain. Why? First of all, because Jesus Christ says so, the apostles say so, and God says so. Jesus Christ said, "Then shall he say also unto them on the left hand, Depart from me, ye cursed, into everlasting fire, prepared for the devil and his angels" (Matthew 25:41). Paul wrote, "The Lord Jesus shall be revealed from heaven with his mighty angels, in flaming fire taking vengeance on them that know not God, and that obey not the gospel of our Lord Jesus Christ: who shall be punished with everlasting destruction from the presence of the Lord, and from the glory of his power" (2 Thessalonians 1:7-9).

John recorded in Revelation 20:15, "Whosoever

was not found written in the book of life was cast into the lake of fire." Peter wrote, "God spared not the angels that sinned, but cast them down to hell, and delivered them unto chains of darkness, to be reserved into judgment; The Lord knoweth how to deliver the godly out of temptations, and to reserve the unjust unto the day of judgment to be punished" (2 Peter 2:4,9).

"The Lord cometh with ten thousands of his saints, to execute judgment upon all, and to convince all that are ungodly among them of all their ungodly deeds which they have ungodly committed, and of all their hard speeches which ungodly sinners have spoken against him" (Jude 14-15).

After Jesus had died and come up again from the abode of the dead, He ascended to the right hand of His Father. He said, "The fearful, and unbelieving, and the abominable, and murderers, and whoremongers, and sorcerers, and idolaters, and all liars, shall have their part in the lake which burneth with fire and brimstone: which is the second death" (Revelation 21:8).

Hell is certain because Jesus Christ and the apostles say it is and because God says it is through them. The only thing against it is the speculation of the theologians and dreams of poets. The words of Christ have stood the test of the centuries and always proved true in the final outcome every time. When I have Christ on one side and speculative theologians on the other, it doesn't take me long to decide which to believe.

Experience, observation, and common sense prove that there is a hell. One of the most certain facts of every man's experience is this—*that where there is sin, there must be suffering.* We all know that. The longer a man continues in sin, the deeper he sinks down into ruin, shame, agony, and despair. There are hundreds and thousands of men and women in the world living in a very practical hell, and the hell is getting worse every day. You may not know how to reconcile what these men and women suffer with the doctrine that God is love. But no intelligent man gives up facts because he cannot explain the philosophy behind them.

Now, if this process keeps going on, sinking ever deeper into ruin, shame, and despair, when the time of possible repentance has passed, what is left but an everlasting hell? The only thing against it is the dreams of poets and the speculations of would-be philosophers. But the speculations of philosophers have proven to be misleading from the dawn of history. When we have the sure teaching of the Word of God, the case is settled.

There is a hell. It is more certain that there is a hell than that you will wake again tomorrow morning. You probably will; you may not. But it is absolutely certain that there is a hell. The next time you buy a book, no matter how skillfully it is written, and that author wants to prove to you that there is no hell, you will have paid to be made a fool of. There is a hell.

Chapter 5

A PICTURE OF HELL

"Fear him which is able to destroy both soul and body in hell"—Matthew 10:28.

We know that hell is a real place, but what is it like? What kind of people are there? Will they really remain in hell forever?

Hell is a place of extreme bodily suffering. That is plain from the teaching of the New Testament. The words commonly used to express the doom of unrepenting sinners are "death" and "destruction."

What do death and destruction mean? God has carefully defined His terms. In Revelation 17:8, we are told that the beast will go into "perdition." The word translated *perdition* is translated elsewhere *destruction.*

In Revelation 19:20, you will read that the beast and the false prophet were cast into "a lake of fire burning with brimstone." One thousand years after the beast and the false prophet have been thrown into the lake of fire, the devil also is cast in. They will be "tormented day and night for ever and ever" (Revelation 20:10). By God's definition, *perdition* or *destruction* is a place in a lake of torment forever.

Now let us look at God's definition of death. "The fearful, and unbelieving, and the abominable, and murderers, and whoremongers, and sorcerers, and idolaters, and all liars, shall have their part in the lake which burneth with fire and brimstone: which is the second death" (Revelation 21:8). God's definition of *death* is a portion in the "lake of fire burning with brimstone," the same as His definition of *perdition*.

"Oh," you may respond, "that is all highly figurative." Remember God's figures stand for facts. When some people come to something unwelcome in the Bible, they will say it is figurative and imagine that they have done away with it. You cannot do away with God's Word by calling it figurative. God is no liar, and God's figures never overstate the facts. Hell means at least this much—bodily suffering of the most intense kind.

Furthermore, in the next life, we do not exist as disembodied spirits. This theory is man's philosophy and not New Testament teaching. According to the Bible, in the world to come, the spirit has a radically different body, but it is the perfect counterpart of the spirit that inhabits it and partakes in punishment or reward.

Even in this life, inward spiritual sin often causes outward bodily pain. Many people are suffering the most severe pain because of inward sin. Hell is the hospital of the incurables of the universe, where men exist in awful and perpetual pain.

Painful Memories

But physical pain is the least significant feature of hell. *Hell is a place of memory and remorse.* In the picture Christ gave us of the rich man in hell, Abraham said to the rich man, "Remember." (See Luke 16:25.) The rich man brought little that he had on earth with him, but he had taken one thing—his memory.

If you choose to go on in sin and spend eternity in hell, you won't take much with you that you own, but you will take your memory. Men will remember the women whose lives they have ruined, and women will remember the time squandered in frivolity, fashion, and foolishness, when they might have been living for God. They will remember the Christ they rejected and the opportunities for salvation they despised.

There is no torment like the torment of an accusing memory. I have seen strong men weeping like children. What was the matter? Memory. One of the strongest, most intelligent men I ever knew threw himself upon the floor of my office and sobbed hysterically. What was the matter? Memory. I have had men and women hurry up to me at the close of a service with pale cheeks and

43

haunted eyes, begging for a private conversation. What was the matter? Memory.

You will take your memory with you. The memory and the conscience that are not set at peace in this life by the atoning blood of Christ and the pardoning grace of God never will be. Hell is the place where men remember and suffer.

When D.L. Moody was a boy, one day he was hoeing corn along with an elderly man. Suddenly, the man stopped hoeing and began striking a stone with his hoe. Young Moody stared at him. Tears were rolling down the man's cheeks, and he said, "Dwight, when I was a lad like you I left home to make a living for myself. As I came out of the front gate, my mother handed me a Bible and said, 'My boy, seek first the Kingdom of God and His righteousness, and all these things shall be added unto you.'"

He took a deep breath and continued, "I went to the next town. I went to church on Sunday, and the minister got up to preach. He announced his text—Matthew 6:33. He looked right down at me, pointed his finger at me, and said, 'Young man, Seek ye first the Kingdom of God and His righteousness, and all these things shall be added unto you.'

"I went out of the church and had an awful struggle! It seemed as if the minister was talking to me. I decided, 'No; I will get settled in life first, and then I will become a Christian.'

"I found no work in that town, but I went to

another town and found a job. I went to church, as was my custom, Sunday after Sunday. After a few Sundays, the minister stood up in the pulpit and announced his text—Matthew 6:33. 'Seek ye first the Kingdom of God and His righteousness, and all these things shall be added unto you.' "

The old man began to tremble violently. "Dwight, he seemed to look right at me and point his finger right at me. I got up and went out of the church. I went to the cemetery behind the church and sat down on a tombstone. I had an awful fight, but at last I said, 'No, I will not become a Christian until I get settled in life.' " He paused for a moment and then said, "Dwight, from that day to this the Spirit of God has left me, and I have never had the slightest inclination to be a Christian."

Mr. Moody said, "I did not understand it then. I was not a Christian myself. I went to Boston and was converted. Then I understood. I wrote to my mother and asked her what had become of the old man. She answered, "Dwight, he has gone insane, and they have taken him to the Brattleboro Insane Asylum."

I went to Brattleboro and called on him there. As I went into his cell, he glared at me, pointed his finger at me, and said, "Young man, seek ye first the Kingdom of God and His righteousness." I could do nothing with him.

I went back to Boston. After some time I came home again. I asked my mother where he was now.

"Oh!" she said, "he is home, but he is a helpless imbecile."

I went up to his house. There he sat in a rocking chair, a white-haired man. As I went into the room, he pointed his finger at me and said, "Young man, seek ye first the Kingdom of God and His righteousness." He had gone crazy with memory. Hell is the madhouse of the universe, where men and women remember.

Desires Forever Denied

Hell is a place of insatiable and tormenting desire. You remember what Jesus tells us of the rich man in hell. The rich man said, "Send Lazarus, that he may dip the tip of his finger in water, and cool my tongue; for I am tormented in this flame" (Luke 16:24).

You will carry into the next world the desires that you build up here. Hell is the place where desire and passion exist in their highest potency, and where there is nothing to gratify them. Men and women who are living in sin and worldliness are developing passions and desires for which there is no gratification in hell. Happy is that man or woman who sets his affection on the things above. Those who cultivate powers, passions, and desires for which there is no gratification in the next world will spend eternity in severe torment.

Hell is a place of shame. Oh, the awful, heartbreaking agony of shame. It can cause depression, illness, and even death. A bank cashier was in a hurry to get rich, so he appropriated the funds of the bank and invested them, intending to pay them back. But his investment failed. For a long time, he managed to conceal his theft from the bank examiner. One day the embezzlement was discovered. The cashier had to acknowledge his crime. He was arrested, tried, and sent to prison.

He had a beautiful wife and a lovely child, a sweet little girl. Some time after his arrest and imprisonment, the little child came home sobbing. "Oh," she said, "Mother, I can never go back to that school again. Send for my books."

Thinking it was some childish whim, the mother said, "Of course you will go back."

"No," the child insisted, "I can never go back. Send for my books."

"Darling, what is the matter?"

She said, "Another little girl said to me today, 'Your father is a thief.' "

Oh, the cruel stab! The mother saw that her child could not go back to school.

The wound was fatal. That fair blossom began to fade. A physician was called, but her illness surpassed all the capacities of his skill. The child grew weaker every day until they laid her upon her bed. The physician said, "Madam, I am powerless in this case. The child's heart has given way with the agony of the wound. Your child will probably die."

The mother went in and said to her dying child,

"Darling, is there anything you would like to have me do for you?"

"Oh," she said, "yes, Mother, send for Father. Let him come home and lay his head down on the pillow beside mine as he used to do."

But the father was behind iron bars. They spoke to the governor, and he said, "I have no power in the matter." They spoke to the warden of the prison. He said, "I have no power in the matter."

But hearts were touched by the girl's condition. The judge and the governor made an arrangement so that the father was permitted to come home under a deputy-warden. He reached his home late at night and entered his house. The physician was waiting. He said, "I think you had better go in tonight, for I am afraid your child will not live until morning."

The father went to the door and opened it. The child looked up quickly. "Oh," she said, "I knew it was you, Father. I knew you would come. Come and lay your head beside mine upon the pillow just as you used to do."

The strong man went and laid his head upon the pillow. The child lovingly patted his cheek and died. She was killed by shame. Hell is the place of shame, where everybody is dishonored.

No Parties In Hell

Hell is a place of vile companionships. The society of hell is described in Revelation 21:8. "The fearful, and unbelieving and the abominable,

48

and murderers, and whoremongers, and sorcerers, and idolaters, and all liars, shall have their part in the lake which burneth with fire and brimstone: which is the second death." Some may say, "Many who are brilliant and gifted are going there." It may be, but how long will it take the most gifted man or woman to sink in such a world as that? I can take you to skid row and show you men who were once physicians, lawyers, congressmen, college professors, leading businessmen, and even ministers of the gospel. But now they are living with thugs, prostitutes, and everything that is vile and bad. How did they get there? They began to sink.

Many years ago, my father was one of the delegates to the Presidential convention in Chicago. We then lived in New York. He took us children to a quiet country town in Michigan and went on to the convention. On the way home, we got on a Hudson River ferry, filled with the leading Democratic politicians. Many gifted orators stood up and spoke to the crowd, but there was one man who eclipsed everyone else. Everybody was spellbound by the power of his eloquence.

Years passed. One day I saw someone lying on our front lawn, covered with vomit, sleeping heavily, snoring like an overfed hog. When I went up to him, I found it was the same man whose gift of speaking had carried away everyone on that ferry. He died in a psychiatric ward from alcoholism.

During the World's Fair, there was a women's

commission appointed to receive the dignitaries and the members of the royalty of other countries. A woman stood near the chairman of the commission, dazzling people by her beauty and wit.

Several years later, some friends of mine were in the slums of Chicago hunting for forlorn people that they might help. They found a poor creature with nails grown like claws, with long, tangled hair twisted full of filth, a face that had not been washed for weeks, clad in a single filthy garment—a wreck! When they began to talk with her, they found it was that woman who had belonged to the women's commission during the World's Fair. She had destroyed herself with cocaine.

A Place Without Hope

Finally, *hell is a world without hope*. There are men who tell you that the Greek word *aionios,* translated "everlasting," never means everlasting. The meaning must be determined by the context. In Matthew 25:46, we read, "And these shall go away into everlasting punishment: but the righteous into life eternal." If it means everlasting in one part of the verse, it must mean the same in the other part of the verse.

There is another expression used often in the Bible—"Unto the ages of the ages." It is used twelve times in one book, eight times describing the existence of God and the duration of His reign, once referring to the duration of the blessedness of the righteous, and in every remaining instance

50

of the punishment of the beast, the false prophet, and the unrepentant. It is the strongest known expression for absolute endlessness.

I have searched my Bible for one ray of hope for men that die without repentance. I have failed after years of search to find one. Scriptures must be carefully interpreted in their context with an honest attempt to discover their true meaning, and not to make them fit a theory.

The New Testament does not contain one ray of hope for men and women who die without Christ. "Forever and ever" is the endless wail of that restless sea of fire. Hell is a place of bodily anguish, a place of agony of conscience, a place of insatiable torment and desire, a place of evil companionship, a place of shame, and a place without hope.

Escape From Hell

There is only one way to escape hell—accept Jesus Christ as your personal Savior, surrender to Him as your Lord and Master, confess Him openly before the world, and live obediently according to His Word. The Bible is perfectly plain about that. "There is none other name under heaven given among men, whereby we must be saved" (Acts 4:12).

"He that believeth on the Son hath everlasting life: and he that believeth not on the Son shall not see life; but the wrath of God abideth on him" (John 3:36).

"Whosoever therefore shall confess me before

men, him will I confess also before my Father which is in heaven. But whosoever shall deny me before men, him will I also deny before my Father which is in heaven'' (Matthew 10:32-33).

"The Lord Jesus shall be revealed from heaven with his mighty angels, in flaming fire taking vengeance on them that know not God, and that obey not the gospel of our Lord Jesus Christ: who shall be punished with everlasting destruction from the presence of the Lord, and from the glory of his power'' (2 Thessalonians 1:7-9).

The question is this—Will you accept Christ now? Hell is too awful to risk it for a year, a month, or even a day. Your eternal destiny may be settled right now.

I know what the devil is whispering to you. He is saying, "Don't be a coward; don't be frightened into repentance." Is it cowardice to be moved by rational fear? Is it heroism to rush into unnecessary danger?

Suppose I looked up and saw a building on fire. A man is sitting near an upper window, reading a book carelessly. I see his peril, and I call out, "Flee for your life! The house is on fire!" Then suppose that man leans out of the window and shouts back, "I am no coward. You can't frighten me." Would he be a hero or a fool?

One night I went to see my parents at home. As I stepped off the train, I stepped on to another track. Unknown to me, an express train was coming down that other track. A man saw my peril and cried, "Mr. Torrey, there is a train coming! Get off the track!" I did not shout back, "I am no coward. You can't scare me." I was not such a fool. I got off the track, or I would not be telling you the story.

You are on the track. I hear the thunder and rumble of the wrath of God as it comes hurrying on, and I cry, "Get off the track!" Receive Christ now!

[Handwritten at top: Why do we always try to blame God for our own doing. If someone goes to hell its not God's fault its there.]

[Handwritten: — did God sin & violate the laws of heaven]
[Handwritten: — did God reject Grace etc~]

Chapter 6

OBSTACLES ON THE ROAD TO HELL

[Handwritten: Hell is the last thing God plans for a human being]

"The Lord. . .is. . .not willing that any should perish, but that all should come to repentance"—2 Peter 3:9.

If any man or woman is lost and goes to hell, it won't be God's fault. If God had His way, every man and woman in the world would be saved at once. God is doing everything in His power to bring you to repentance.

Of course, He cannot save you if you will not repent. You can have salvation if you want to be saved from sin, but sin and salvation can never go together. There are people who talk about a scheme of salvation where man can continue in sin and yet be saved. It is impossible. Sin is damnation, and if a man will go on everlastingly in sin, he will be everlastingly lost.

But God is doing everything in His power to turn you out of the path of sin and destruction into the path of righteousness and everlasting life. God has filled the path of sin—the path that leads to

[Handwritten in left margin, rotated: Some people just don't want to & they send themselves to hell]

54

hell—with obstacles. He has made it hard and bitter.

A great many people are saying today, "The Christian life is so hard." It is not. Jesus said, "For my yoke is easy, and my burden is light" (Matthew 11:30). God tells us in His Word, "The way of transgressors is hard" (Proverbs 13:15). God has filled it full of obstacles, and you cannot go on in it without surmounting one obstacle after another.

The Power In God's Word

The first obstacle is *the Bible*. You cannot get very far in the path of sin without finding the Bible in your way. The Bible is one of the greatest hindrances to sin in the world. It contains warnings, invitations, and descriptions of the character and consequences of sin. It gives us representations of righteousness, its beauty and its reward. With its pictures of God and God's love, the Bible always stands as a great hindrance to sin. That is the reason many men hate the Bible. They are determined to sin, and the Bible makes them uneasy in sin, so they hate the Book.

Men sometimes say to me, "I object to the Bible because of its filthy stories." But when I look into their lives, I find that their lives are filthy. The Bible paints sin in its true colors with stories that make sin hideous. Their objection is not to the stories, but because the Bible makes them uneasy in their filthy lives.

A man has often been turned back from the path

of sin by a single verse in the Bible. Hundreds have been turned out of the path of sin by Romans 6:23, "The wages of sin is death; but the gift of God is eternal life through Jesus Christ our Lord." Thousands have been turned out of the path of sin by Amos 4:12, "Prepare to meet thy God." Tens of thousands have been turned out of the path of sin by John 3:16, "For God so loved the world, that he gave his only begotten Son, that whosoever believeth in him should not perish, but have everlasting life." John 6:37 contains the promise, "Him that cometh to me I will in no wise cast out."

Several years ago a man who had not been in a house of worship for fifteen years came into our church in Chicago. He was a strong agnostic and proud of it. I don't know why he came in that night. I suppose he saw the crowd coming and was curious to know what was going on. He sat down, and I began to preach. In my sermon, I quoted John 6:37, "Him that cometh to me I will in no wise cast out." It went like an arrow into that man's heart.

When the meeting was over, he got up and went out and tried to forget that verse, but could not. He went to bed but could not sleep. "Him that cometh to me I will in no wise cast out" kept ringing in his mind. The next day it haunted him at work, and for days and weeks that verse troubled him, but he refused to come to Christ. He came back to the street where our church stands, walked up and down the sidewalk, stamped his foot, and cursed the text, but he could not get rid of it.

Six weeks had passed when he came into our prayer meeting. He stood up and said, "I was here six weeks ago and heard your minister preach. I heard the text, John 6:37, and I have tried to forget it, but it has haunted me night and day. I have walked up and down the sidewalk in front of your church and cursed the text, but I can't get rid of it. Pray for me." We did, and he was saved. One text from God's Word turned him out of the path of sin and ruin.

The Miracle Of A Mother's Prayers

The second obstacle that God has put in the path of sin is *a mother's holy influence and teaching*. Hundreds of men and women who are not yet Christians have tried to be unbelievers and plunge down into sin. But their mother's holy influence and Christian teaching won't let them go. Sometimes it is years later that a mother's teaching does its work.

A young fellow went west to Colorado to work in the mines. He worked during the day and gambled at night, but he spent more money gambling than he made in the mines. One night he was at the gambling table. He lost his last cent. Then he used some of his employer's money and lost that. He felt he was ruined. He rose from the table, went up into the mountains, drew his revolver, and held it to his temple. He was about to pull the trigger when a word that his mother had spoken to him years before came to his mind. "My son, if you are ever in trouble, think of God." And there, standing in the moonlight, with a revolver pressed against his temple, and his finger upon the trigger, he remembered what his mother had said and dropped on his knees. He cried to God and was saved.

Another obstacle that God has put in the path of sin and ruin is *a mother's prayers*. In the desperate hardness of our hearts, we often trample our mother's teaching underfoot, but we find it very hard to get over her prayers. Often at the last moment, a man is saved by his mother's prayers.

In my church in Chicago, a man used to stand outside with a container of beer. As the people came out of the meeting, he offered them a drink. He was hard, desperate, and wicked, but he had a praying mother in Scotland.

One night after he went home from the meeting where he had caused trouble, he was awakened and saved without getting out of bed. He came back to Scotland to see his mother. He had a brother who was a sailor in the China seas, and the mother and the saved son knelt down and prayed for the wandering boy. That same night while they prayed, the Spirit of God came down upon that sailor, and he was saved. He later became a missionary to India—a man saved by a mother's prayers.

When I was rushing headlong in the path of sin and ruin, my mother's prayers arose, and I could not get over them. I used to think that nobody had anything to do with my salvation. I had gone to bed one night with no more thought of becoming a Christian than I had of jumping over the moon. In the middle of the night, I climbed out of bed and decided to end my miserable life, but something came upon me. I dropped on my knees. In five minutes from the time I got out of bed to take my life, I had surrendered to God.

I thought no one had anything to do with it. But I found out later that my mother was 427 miles away praying. Although I had gotten over sermons, arguments, churches, and everything else, I could not get over my mother's prayers. Do you know why some men are not in hell tonight? Their mother's prayers have kept them out of hell.

Faithful Preaching And Teaching

Christian witness faithful w/ God's word

Another obstacle on the road to hell is *the sermons we hear.* How many thousands of people are turned back from sin to God by sermons that they hear or read. Sometimes the sermon does its work years later.

Pastor's sermon

In my first pastorate, I prepared a sermon on the parable of the ten virgins. There was one member of my congregation who was very much on my heart. I prayed she might be saved by that sermon. I went and preached; but when I gave the invitation, she never made a sign. I went home and did not know what to make of it. I said, "I prayed for her conversion by that sermon and fully expected her conversion, but she is not converted."

Years later, when I had gone to another pastorate, I heard that this woman was converted. I revisited the place, called upon her, and said, "I am very glad to hear you have been converted."

She said, "Would you like to know how I was converted?" I said I would. "Do you remember preaching a sermon years ago on the ten virgins? I could not get your words out of my mind. I felt I must take Christ that night, but I would not. That sermon followed me, and I was converted years later by it."

Another obstacle is a *Sunday school teacher's influence and teaching.* A faithful Sunday school teacher is one of God's best instruments on earth for the salvation of the perishing.

In Mr. Moody's first Sunday school in Chicago, he had a class of very unruly girls. Nobody could manage them. Finally, he found a young man who could keep the class under control. One day this young man came to Mr. Moody and said, "Mr. Moody," as he suddenly burst into tears.

Mr. Moody said, "What is the matter?"

"The doctor says I have tuberculosis, and that I must go to California at once or die." He sobbed as if his heart would break.

Mr. Moody tried to comfort him and said, "Suppose that is true, you have no reason to feel so bad. You are a Christian."

"It is not that, Mr. Moody; I am perfectly willing to die, but I have had this Sunday school class all these years and not one of them is saved. I am going off to leave them, every one unsaved." He sobbed like a child.

Mr. Moody said, "Wait, I will get a carriage, and we will drive around and visit them. One by one you can lead them to Christ."

He took the pale teacher in the carriage, and they drove around to the homes of the girls. He talked to them about Christ until he was so tired that he had to be taken home. The next day they went out again, and they went out every day until every one of these women but one was saved. They met for a prayer meeting before he went away. One after another led in prayer, and at last the one unsaved girl prayed too and accepted Christ.

He left by the early train the next morning, and Mr. Moody went to see him off. As they were waiting, one by one the girls came to say goodbye. He spoke a few words of farewell to them. As the train pulled out of the station, he stood upon the back platform of the car with his finger pointing heavenward, telling his Sunday school class to meet him in heaven.

Kindness Is Never Wasted

Sometimes God throws *a kind word or an act* as an obstacle in the path of sin. A lady was standing at a window looking out on a New York street. A drunkard came down the street. He had been the mayor of a Southern city, but now he was a penniless drunkard on the streets of New York. He had made up his mind to commit suicide. He started for the river, but then he thought, "I will go into a bar and have one more drink. I have spent a lot of money in that bar, and I can certainly get one drink without paying for it."

He went in and asked for a drink and told the man he had no money. The man came around from behind the bar and threw him out into the street.

The woman who was looking out of the window saw the poor man picking himself up out of the gutter. She hurried over to him, wiped the mud off his face with her handkerchief, and said, "Come over to our meeting. It is bright and warm, and you will be welcome." He followed her over and sat on the bench. The meeting began, and one after another gave their testimony. After the meeting, that lady came and spoke to him about his soul. His heart was touched, and he was saved.

He got a job, and then a better one, and finally was made manager of one of the largest publishing houses in New York City. One day he came to the woman who had found him in the gutter and said, "I have some friends at a hotel that I want you to meet." She went to the hotel, and he introduced her to a fine-looking, middle-aged woman and a lovely young lady. He said, "This is my wife and daughter"—beautiful, refined, cultured ladies whom he had left and gone down to the gates of hell. But a kind act and a word of invitation to

Christ reached him and placed him on the path that leads to glory. Oh, let us go as the missionaries of God's grace and block the path of sinful men and women with kind deeds and turn them to righteousness and to God.

The Voice Of The Spirit

Another obstacle that God puts in the path of sin and ruin is *the Holy Spirit*. You and I have experienced the Holy Spirit's working, perhaps without realizing it. Perhaps we were right in the midst of a party, when a strange feeling came into our heart. It was a feeling of unrest, dissatisfaction with the life we were living, or a longing for something better. The feeling would be accompanied by memories of home, church, mother, Bible, and God.

One night a man was at a gambling table. He was a wild, reckless, spendthrift. Suddenly the voice of God's Spirit spoke to his heart. He thought he was about to die. He sprang up from the table, threw down his cards, and rushed to his room. There was someone in the room. He thought at first, "I won't pray while the maid is in the room." But he was so much in earnest that he did not care what anybody might think. He dropped down by his bed and called upon God for Christ's sake to forgive his sins. The man was Brownlow North. He did a great work for God in Ireland and Scotland in the 1800's.

If you have ever been in a nightclub when there

came into your heart a wretchedness, a sense of disgust, a longing for something better, a calling to a purer life, that was God's Spirit. If you have ever felt a stirring in your heart, you might have said to yourself, "I wonder if I had better become a Christian now?" God is sending His Spirit to block the road to hell. Listen to God's Spirit. Yield and accept Christ.

Facing The Cross

God has put one other obstacle in the road as a blockade in the path to hell—that is *the cross of Christ*. No man can get very far down the path of sin and ruin before he sees the cross looming before him. On that cross hangs a Man, the Son of Man, the Son of God. You see Him hanging with nails in His hands and feet, and a voice says, "It was for you. I bore this for you. I died for you." In the pathway of every man and woman stands the cross with Christ upon it. If you choose to continue in sin, you will have to step over the cross and over the crucified form of the Son of God.

I heard of a godly old man who had a worthless son. That son was more anxious to make money than he was for honor or anything else. He decided to go into the liquor business.

Any man who is willing to make money out of selling alcoholic beverages will profit from the tears of broken-hearted wives and the groans and sighs of an alcoholic's sons and daughters. The abuse of liquor is sending thousands of men every year to premature graves. It causes more sorrow, more ruined homes, more wretchedness than perhaps anything else on earth. Every tavern owner, every bartender, every barmaid, and every professed Christian that holds stocks in breweries or distilleries is a part of the crime.

Once I knew of a man who was going to open a tavern. His father was deeply grieved and tried to reason with his son. He said, "My boy, you bear an honorable name which has never been disgraced before. Don't disgrace it by putting it up over a bar." But the son was so determined to get rich that he would not listen to his father.

The day came to open the bar. The father was one of the first on hand. He stepped up to every man that approached the door and told him of the miseries that came from alcohol. One after another, they turned away. The son looked out of the window to see why he was getting no customers. He saw his father outside, turning his customers away. He came outside and said, "Father, go home. You are ruining my business."

He said, "I can't help it, my boy. I won't have my name dishonored by this business. If you are determined to go on with it, I will stand here and warn every man that comes to enter your door."

Finally, the son lost his temper. He struck his old father in the face. The father turned to him without any anger. He said, "My son, you can strike me if you will. You can kill me if you will, but no man will enter your bar unless he goes over my dead body.''

No man or woman will ever enter hell unless they go over the dead body of Jesus Christ. No man or woman can refuse Christ and persist in sin without trampling underfoot the One who was crucified on the cross of Calvary for us.

God has piled the obstacles high in His patient love! Don't try to surmount them. Turn back. Turn away from the path of sin; turn toward the path of faith in Jesus Christ. Turn now!

Great last story.
Obstacle is the crucified
Christ, all come face to face
w/ him at one time or another
& if they are going to go to hell
they must step over his
dead body, & ignore him

Chapter 7

CATCHING A GLIMPSE OF HEAVEN

"He looked for a city which hath foundations, whose builder and maker is God"—Hebrews 11:10.

"Here have we no continuing city, but we seek one to come"—Hebrews 13:14.

Heaven was the city Abraham sought, the "city which hath foundations." This is "the continuing city" which we are seeking instead of these fleeting and perishable cities and homes of earth. What sort of a place is this city? What sort of a place is heaven?

In answer to the question, I am not going to discuss the sort of a place I imagine heaven to be. I care very little about my speculations or any other man's speculations and fancies on this point. I am going to tell you something that is certain. I am going to tell you what God plainly teaches in His Word.

There are many who think we know nothing about heaven, and that it is all guesswork. That is not so. God has revealed much about it. What He has revealed is very encouraging. It will awaken in every wise and true heart a desire to go there.

If we reflected more about heaven, it would help us to bear our burdens here more bravely. We would want to live holier lives and be delivered from the power of greed and lust that often attacks us. Our lives would be filled with joy and sunshine.

Shallow philosophers tell us that our business is to live this present life and let the future take care of itself. You might as well tell the schoolboy that his business is to live today without considering his future. True thoughts of the life that is to come clothe the life that now is with new beauty and strength.

The Reality Of Heaven

Jesus said, "I go to prepare a place for you" (John 14:2). Some will tell you that heaven is merely a state or condition. Doubtless it is more important to be in a heavenly state or condition than in a heavenly place. But heaven is a real place. We are not to be merely in a heavenly state of mind, but in a heavenly city as well, "a city that hath foundations," "a continuing city."

Christ has already entered into heaven to appear in the presence of God for us. (See Hebrews 9:24.) He has gone to prepare a place for us and is coming back to take us there. We will not be disembodied spirits in the world to come, but redeemed spirits, in redeemed bodies, in a redeemed universe.

Heaven is a place of incomparable beauty. This is obvious from the description we have in Revelation 21 and 22. The God of the Bible is a God of beauty. He made this world beautiful. Its beauty has been marred by sin. The weed, the thorn, and the brier spring up. The insect devours the roses, and the lilies fade. Decay and death bring loathsome sights and foul smells.

All of creation, together with fallen man, groans and travails in pain until now. But enough is left of the original creation to show us how intensely God loves beauty. He has told us in His Word that the creation will be delivered from the bondage of corruption into the glorious liberty of the children of God. (See Romans 8:20-23.)

There will be perfection of beauty in heaven. Perfection of form, color, and sound will be combined into a beauty that will be indescribable. All earthly comparisons fail. Every sense of perception in our present state is clouded by sin. But in our redemption bodies, every sense will be enlarged and exist in perfection.

Some of us have seen beautiful visions on earth. We have seen the mountains rearing their snow-crowned heads through the clouds; the vista of rolling hills and verdant valleys; winding rivers and forests with their changing colors; the lake and ocean dancing and tossing and rolling in the moonlight; the heavens in the clear wintry night jewelled with countless stars. We have caught the fragrances that float through the summer night in parks and gardens. We have listened to the indescribable harmonies of piano and violin as they responded to the touch of the master's hand and the more matchless music of the human voice. But all these are nothing compared to the beauty of sight and sound and fragrance that will greet us in that fair city of eternity.

The Best Companions

But the beauty of heaven, as good and attractive as it is, will be its least important characteristic. Heaven will be a place of high and holy companionships. The best, wisest, and noblest men of all ages will be there. Abraham and Isaac and Jacob will be there. "And I say unto you, That many shall come from the east and west, and shall sit down with Abraham, and Isaac, and Jacob, in the kingdom of heaven" (Matthew 8:11). Heaven is the home of Moses, Elijah, Daniel, Paul, John, Rutherford, and Brainerd. All the purest, noblest, most unselfish people the world has known are there because they have trusted in the atoning blood of Christ.

"For we know that if our earthly house of this tabernacle were dissolved, we have a building of God, an house not made with hands, eternal in the heavens" (2 Corinthians 5:1). All the dear ones who believed in and loved the Lord Jesus will be there.

There are many who desire to get into the most exclusive social circles. That is all right if it is not merely the society of wealth, fashion, and foolishness that is so strangely called "the best society." But the most select group of this world will be nothing compared to the society of heaven. The joys we find in the companionship of noble, unselfish, thoughtful people here give only the faintest conception of the joys of heaven's companionships.

The angels are there. "And the angel answering said unto him, I am Gabriel, that stand in the presence of God; and am sent to speak unto thee, and to shew thee these glad tidings" (Luke 1:19).

"I say unto you, that likewise joy shall be in heaven over one sinner that repenteth, more than over ninety and nine just persons, which need no repentance. . . .Likewise, I say unto you, there is joy in the presence of the angels of God over one sinner that repenteth" (Luke 15:7,10). We will enjoy the companionship of these lofty beings—Gabriel, Michael, and the whole angelic host.

God Himself is there, too. In a sense, He is everywhere, but heaven is the place of His peculiar presence and manifestation of Himself. "Then hear thou from heaven thy dwelling place" (2 Chronicles 6:30). "Thy kingdom come. Thy will be done in earth, as it is in heaven" (Matthew 6:10).

We will hold communion with Him. Jesus Christ is there. "And said, Behold, I see the heavens opened, and the Son of man standing on the right hand of God" (Acts 7:56). "Seeing then that we have a great high priest, that is passed into the heavens, Jesus the Son of God, let us hold fast our profession" (Hebrews 4:14). "Now of the things which we have spoken this is the sum: We have such an high priest, who is set on the right hand of the throne of the Majesty in the heavens" (Hebrews 8:1).

To Paul, being with Jesus was one of the most attractive thoughts about heaven. "For I am in a straight betwixt two, having a desire to depart, and be with Christ; which is far better: Nevertheless to abide in the flesh is more needful for you" (Philippians 1:23-24).

There will be no unpleasant or degrading companions in heaven. The devil will not be there. The lewd, the vulgar, and the obscene will not be there. The greedy and the scheming and selfish will not be there. The liar, the slanderer, the backbiter, the meddler, and the gossip will not be there. The mean, the contemptible, and the hypocrite will not be there. The profane, the blasphemer, and the scoffer will not be there. No money, influence, or cunning will get them in. "And there shall in no wise enter into it any thing that defileth, neither whatsoever worketh abomination, or maketh a lie" (Revelation 21:27).

There are limitations to the joys of the dearest earthly companionships. It will not be so in heaven. We can perfectly open our hearts to one another there, as we often long to do here but are unable. "For now we see through a glass, darkly; but then face to face: now I know in part; but then shall I know even as also I am known" (1 Corinthians 13:12).

Heaven will be a place of glad reunions. "Then we which are alive and remain shall be caught up together with them in the clouds, to meet the Lord in the air: and so shall we ever be with the Lord" (1 Thessalonians 4:17). The bereaved wife will meet again the husband she has missed so long, and the son will see the mother whose departure left his life so desolate. What glad days those coming days will be when we meet again never more to part.

The Most Glorious Freedom

Heaven will be a place that is free from everything that curses or mars our life here. The world we live in would be a happy place if there was no sin, sickness, pain, poverty, or death. But these things ruin the present world.

There will be none of these things in heaven. There will be no sin. Everyone will perfectly obey the will of God. There will be no poverty. Everyone will have all the inexhaustible wealth of God at his disposal. "And if children, then heirs; heirs of God, and joint-heirs with Christ; if so be that we suffer with him, that we may be also glorified together" (Romans 8:17).

There will be no grinding labor. When I see the

73

men and women who rise at dawn and go forth to another day of backbreaking labor, I rejoice that there is a place where the weary can rest. "There remaineth therefore a rest to the people of God" (Hebrews 4:9).

There will be no sickness or pain. "And God shall wipe away all tears from their eyes; and there shall be no more death, neither sorrow, nor crying, neither shall there be any more pain: for the former things are passed away" (Revelation 21:4). There will be no more aching limbs, no more throbbing temples, and no more darting pains. Weakness, sighs, groans, nights of tossing in sweltering rooms, and tears will become vague memories from a distant past. There will be no death in heaven.

Heaven will be a place of universal and perfect knowledge. On this earth, the wisest of us sees through a glass darkly, but there face to face. Here we know in part, but there we will know even as we are known. (See 1 Corinthians 13:12.) The wisest scientist or philosopher on earth knows very little. Sir Isaac Newton said to one who praised his wisdom, "I am as a child on the seashore picking up a pebble here and a shell there, but the great ocean of truth still lies before me."

In heaven the most uneducated of us will have fathomed that great ocean of truth. We will have perfect knowledge of all things. The great perplexing problems of God and man, of time and eternity will be solved. No doubts, no questions, no uncertainties, or errors will trouble us. Faith will be swallowed up in sight.

Heaven will be a place of universal and perfect love. "Beloved, now are we the sons of God, and it doth not yet appear what we shall be: but we know that, when he shall appear, we shall be like him; for we shall see him as he is" (1 John 3:2). We shall be like our God, and He is love. "He that loveth not, knoweth not God; for God is love" (1 John 4:8).

What a place to live, where everyone is a lover and where all love is perfect. How happy is the home where love is triumphant. It may be a very plain place, but it is a happy place. "Better is a dinner of herbs where love is, than a stalled ox and hatred therewith" (Proverbs 17:8).

All is love in heaven. And the love there will not be like that of earth—hesitating, suspicious, selfish, now so cold and then so warm. It will be pure, unbounded, unfaltering, unchanging, and Christlike. What a world that will be! The universal brotherhood of which we read and talk so much and see so little will find its perfect realization there.

Heaven will be a place of praise. "After this I beheld, and, lo, a great multitude, which no man could number, of all nations, and kindreds, and people, and tongues, stood before the throne, and before the Lamb, clothed with white robes, and palms in their hands; And cried with a loud voice, saying, Salvation to our God which sitteth upon the throne, and unto the Lamb. And all the angels stood round about the throne, and about the elders and the four beasts, and fell before the throne on their faces, and worshipped God, Saying, Amen: Blessing, and glory, and wisdom, and thanksgiving, and honour, and power, and might, be unto our God for ever and ever. Amen" (Revelation 7:9-12).

Men will have open eyes to see God as He is. Souls will burst forth with praise. Suppose we should get one glimpse of God as He is, one view of Jesus Christ as He is! There would be a burst of song like the world has never heard.

There will be melody all day long in heaven. Some people ask me in a critical way, "Why do you have so much music in your evangelistic meetings?" I answered, "Because we wish them to be as much like heaven as possible." Heaven will be a very musical place. There will be far more singing than preaching there.

Heaven will be "a city which hath foundations," a "continuing city" (See Hebrews 11:10; 13:14.) Earth's greatest cities and fairest homes do not abide—they crumble into dust. The so-called "eternal city" of the past is trodden underneath the feet of the beggars of modern Rome.

The world itself does not abide. "The world passeth away" (1 John 2:17). Heaven does abide. Eternity rolls on, but heaven abides in its beauty, glory, joy, and love; and we abide with it.

The Way To Heaven

Is your heart stirred with a longing for that abiding city? Who would not rather have an entrance there than to have the fleeting possessions of any of earth's millionaires? If I had my choice between having all that money could buy, and then missing heaven in the end, and living in the most wretched tenement but gaining heaven at last, it would not take long to decide which to choose.

When we reach that fair home, the trials of earth will seem small and trifling indeed. "I reckon that the sufferings of this present time are not worthy to be compared with the glory which shall be revealed in us" (Romans 8:18).

We may all gain an entrance there. There is but one way, but it is simple and open to all. In John 14:6, "Jesus saith unto them, I am the way, the truth, and the life: no man cometh unto the Father, but by me." In John 10:9, He says, "I am the door: by me if any man enter in, he shall be saved, and shall go in and out, and find pasture."

Christ is the door to heaven; Christ is the way to God. Accept Christ as your Savior, your Master, and your Lord. Do it now. If you stood outside the door of some fair mansion where all inside was beauty and love, and the owner said cordially, "Come in," would you risk waiting for a second invitation? Jesus swings heaven's door open wide and says, "Come in." Accept Him at once and gain a right to enter and live forever in heaven.

There was a godless father who had a sweet little child who was an earnest Christian. The young daughter became ill and died. The father was very angry at God. After the funeral he raged about his room cursing God and blaming Him for taking his beloved child. At last, utterly worn out, he threw himself upon the bed and fell asleep.

In his slumber, he dreamed that he stood beside a dark river. He saw a beautiful land on the far side. As he gazed across the river, he saw children coming toward him. One fair child came forth, whom he recognized as his little daughter. She was beckoning to him and calling, "Come over here, Father! Come over here."

He awoke and burst into tears. He gave up his rebellion against God, accepted Christ, and prepared to meet his child in the fair land beyond the river.

There are voices of loved ones who have gone before calling, "Come over here, Father;" "Come over here, Son;" "Come over here, Husband;" "Come over here, Wife." Accept Christ at once and gain the right to enter heaven and live there forever.

Chapter 8

THE NEW BIRTH

"Ye must be born again"—John 3:7.

No one can be saved unless he is born again by the power of God's Holy Spirit. Jesus said, "Ye must be born again." The necessity is absolute. He did not merely say, "Ye may be born again if you think that you want to be," but "Ye *must* be born again."

Nothing else will take the place of the new birth. Neither baptism nor confirmation can be substituted for it. Simon, in the eighth chapter of Acts, was baptized and taken into the early Church. But when Peter and John came down and saw his heart, Peter said to him, "Thou hast neither lot nor part in this matter: for thy heart is not right in the sight of God. . . .Thou art in the gall of bitterness, and in the bond of iniquity" (Acts 8:21,23). He was a baptized, lost sinner!

I often ask people to come to Christ, but they say, "I have been baptized; I have been confirmed." Have you been born again? "Ye must be born again."

No performance of religious duties will take the place of the new birth. A great many people are depending upon the fact that they say their prayers, read their Bibles, go to church, receive communion, and perform other duties. But all of that will not take the place of the new birth. "Ye must be born again."

No Substitutes

Strict adherence to faith will not take the place of the new birth. A great many people are saying, "I believe the Apostles' Creed; I hold the right views about Christ, the right views about the Bible, the right views about the atonement."

You can be orthodox upon every doctrine and still be lost forever. The devil is as orthodox a person as there is. The devil knows the truth about the Bible. He hates it and loves to get others to believe something else, but he believes it himself. The devil knows the truth about Christ. He believes in the divinity of Christ. He tries to keep others from believing in it, but he believes in it himself. The devil believes the truth about hell. No one knows better than the devil that there is an everlasting hell. The devil is perfectly orthodox, but he is lost. "Ye must be born again."

Culture, refinement, and outward morality will not take the place of the new birth. The trouble with us is not merely in our outward life. The trouble is in the heart. The corruption is in the heart, in the very depths of our inner life. Merely to reform your outward life will not save you. It does not go deep enough.

Suppose I had a rotten apple. I could take that apple to an artist and have him put a coating of wax around it, and then paint it until it was beautiful in appearance. But it would be just as rotten as ever. If you would take one bite of it, you would bite into the decay.

Without Christ, people are rotten at the heart. Mere culture, refinement, respectability, and reform simply put a coating of wax on the outside. We must be changed down to the depths of our being. We need the power of God going down to the deepest depths of our souls, banishing death and bringing in life; banishing corruption and bringing in the holiness of God.

Without holiness, no man shall see God. (See Hebrews 12:14.) It is only by the regenerating power of the Spirit of God that any man or woman can become holy. "Ye must be born again."

The necessity of the new birth is universal. No one will ever see the Kingdom of God unless he is born again. There is no exception. I do not care how refined, how highly educated, how amiable, or attractive you are. You will never see the Kingdom of God unless you are born again.

If anybody could have entered the Kingdom of God without the new birth it was Nicodemus. Nicodemus was an upright man and honored by everyone. He moved in the best society as a man of wealth and culture. He belonged to the orthodox party, a man of deep religious earnestness, sincerely desiring to know the right way. He prayed and studied his Bible and went to the synagogue several times a week. The Lord Jesus looked him right in the face, and He said, "Nicodemus, you must be born again." No exceptions.

Have you been born again? I do not ask if you are a church member or if you believe the truth. I do not ask if you say your prayers or read your Bible. I do not ask if you go to church. I do not ask if you have a liberal heart toward the poor or if you give to foreign missions. Have you been born again?

"Born Again" Defined

What does it mean to be born again? A good definition is given in 2 Corinthians 5:17, "If any man be in Christ, he is a new creature: old things are passed away; behold, all things are become new."

The new birth is a new creation. It involves a radical transformation by the power of the Spirit of God in the depths of our being. We receive a new will, new affections, and new thoughts. We were born with a perverted will, corrupted affections, and a blinded mind. In regeneration by the power of the Holy Spirit, God transforms our will, our affections, and our tastes. He transforms our way of looking at things.

Every man and woman by nature has a perverted will that is set on pleasing self. What pleases us may not be evil in itself. Perhaps we do not get drunk or swear or lie or do anything vicious or vulgar. But our minds are bent on pleasing ourselves.

When God, by His Spirit, imparts to us His nature and life, our will is changed along with the whole purpose of our life. Instead of pleasing self, our will is surrendered to God, and we live to please Him. We may do a great many of the things we did before, but now we do them because they please God.

Our affections are corrupt by nature. We love the things we should not love and hate the things we should love. For example, a great many women love to read romantic novels more than they love to read the Bible. If a great many Christian women told the truth they would say, "I would rather read a good love story any day of the week than read the Bible."

You love to go to nightclubs which God hates. I don't say God hates the people in the night-clubs—He loves them; but He hates the night-clubs. Perhaps you would rather go to the theater than to the gathering of God's children. If you had your choice between going to a first-class opera or to a place where God's Spirit was present in power, would you choose the opera? Would you go to a card party rather than to a quiet gathering of God's people where they knelt down and prayed for the outpouring of the Spirit?

When God, through the power of the Spirit, gives you a new nature, you will love the Bible more than any other book in the world. You will love the place where God manifests Himself better than any place of worldly entertainment. You will love the company of God's people better than you will love the pleasures of this world. The beautiful thing is that in a moment of time, by the power of God's Holy Spirit, the change comes. New tastes and new affections take the place of the old tastes and old affections.

All Things Become New

Nobody loves worldly entertainment more than I once did. I used to attend four to six dances a week. I played cards every day of my life except on Sundays. You could not pay me to do these things today. I would never go to a nightclub unless I went there to get some poor soul out. I love the things I once hated, and I hate the things I once loved. In those days I would rather have read any novel than read the Bible. Today I have more joy in reading this Book than in any other book on earth. I love it. My greatest intellectual joy is to study the wonderful pages of this Book of God.

Many people are blind to the divine authority of the Bible. You believe all the nonsense that people try to tell you about the contradictions in it. When you are born again, your mind will be so in tune with the mind of God that you will believe everything His Word says, in spite of everybody.

Some people cannot believe that Jesus took our sins in His own body on the cross. The preaching of this doctrine is foolishness to them that perish. (See 1 Corinthians 1:18.) But when you are born again, the doctrine that the Son of God died on the cross of Calvary will be one of the sweetest doctrines in all the universe.

Being born again means having a new will set on pleasing God instead of pleasing self. You will have new affections to love the things that God loves and to hate the things that God hates. Your mind and heart will believe the truth of God.

Have you been born again? If not, you are not saved. "Verily, verily, I say unto thee, Except a man be born again, he cannot see the kingdom of God" (John 3:3).

How can we tell whether we have been born again or not? "Every one that doeth righteousness is born of him" (1 John 2:29). If you have been born of God, you will do as God does. God does righteousness. If you are born of God, righteousness will be the practice of your life.

To do righteousness means to do the things that are right in God's sight. A man that is born of God will study the Word of God to find out what God's will is as revealed in His Word. When he finds out, he will do it. Are you studying the Word of God daily to find out what God wants you to do? When

85

you find out what God wants you to do, are you doing it?

"Whosoever is born of God doth not commit sin" (1 John 3:9). That is, he does not make a practice of sin. To commit sin is to do something you know to be contrary to God's will. The man of God will not, when he knows God's will, disobey it. He may make mistakes. He may do something that he did not think was against God's will. But when he learns that it was wrong, he will confess it as sin. Or he may be overtaken by a sudden temptation and fall. But as soon as he sees it, he will confess it. He will not go on day after day doing that which he knows to be contrary to the will of God. Anybody that is making a practice of something that they know is contrary to the will of God has reason to doubt whether they are born again.

A young man stopped me on the street and asked, "If a man is born again and lives and dies in sin, will he be saved?"

"Why," I said, "a man who is born again will not live in sin. He may fall into it, but he will not stay there."

Do you know the difference between a hog and a sheep? A hog will fall into the mud, and he will stay there. A sheep may fall into the mud, but he gets up as quickly as he can. Many people that we think are Christ's sheep are only washed hogs. A hog that is washed will return to the mire, but a sheep will not stay in the mud. (See 2 Peter 2:22.)

If you are only outwardly reformed and externally converted, in a few weeks you will go back to your sin and your worldliness. You are only a washed hog. The person who is outwardly converted, but not inwardly transformed, will give up after a little while. But if you have been born again, you are transformed from a hog into a sheep, and you will never lie down in sin again.

The Test Of Love

Proof of regeneration is the love of the brethren. "We know that we have passed from death unto life, because we love the brethren" (1 John 3:14). Our love should include everybody that belongs to Christ, regardless of their social position, race, or color. The nature of God is love, and if God has imparted His nature to you, you have a heart full of love.

I once went to a communion service where the church was receiving new members. When the people stood up to receive the new members, a lady near me remained seated. When the meeting was over I said to her, "Why didn't you stand up to receive the new members?"

She replied, "I was not going to stand up for them. They are our charity cases. I am not going to love and watch over and care for them."

They were poor, and she was rich. She loved rich Christians. A child of God will love the poorest person that is born of God just as much as if he were a millionaire.

Practical love shows itself by reaching into the pocket. People will get up in a prayer meeting sometimes and say, "I know I have passed from death to life because I love the brethren." After the meeting, someone says, "Mrs. Smith is in trouble. She needs a little help, and we are taking up a collection for her. Won't you give something?" The reply is, "I cannot do it. Christmas is coming, and I have got to get presents for my sisters, children, and cousins, and I cannot give to everybody." You can if you are a child of God.

The proof of the new birth is love. If you have a penny left in your pocket, you will go and share it with your poor brothers and sisters, if you are born again.

"Whosoever believeth that Jesus is the Christ is born of God" (1 John 5:1). You say, "I believe that Jesus is the Christ." Do you? It is not mere religion, it is true belief. "Christ" means King. If you believe in Christ as King, you will set Him up as King in your heart. Does Christ sit upon the throne of your heart? Does Christ rule your life? If He does, you are born of God. If He doesn't, you are not.

"Whatsoever is born of God overcometh the world" (1 John 5:4). There are two classes of people in the world—those who are overcoming the world, and those who are being overcome by the world. Which class do you belong to? Are you getting the victory over the world, or is the world getting the victory over you?

A great many people come to me and say, "I know this is not right, but it is what everybody does, and so I do it." The world is getting the victory over you. If you are born of God, you will get the victory over the world. You won't ask what the world does. You will ask what Christ says, and you will obey Christ, your King, and get the victory over the world, even if you have to stand alone.

How To Be Born Again

God tells us exactly what we must do to be born again. "As many as *received* him, to them gave he power to become the sons of God" (John 1:12). We are born again by God's Holy Spirit, through His Word, the moment we receive Christ. When you take Christ into your heart, you take the life of God into your heart. Christ comes and reigns and transforms you completely in a moment. It does not matter how worldly you are, how sinful you are, or how unbelieving you are. Anyone can throw his heart open and let Jesus come in to rule and reign. Anyone can take Christ as his Savior and Deliverer from the power of sin. The moment you surrender the control of your life to Him, God, by the power of His Holy Spirit, will make you a new creature.

Let us compare two persons—one who has been carefully taught to observe the outward forms of Christianity, and another who has gone down into the depths of sin. We may look at the religious person and say, "She will surely be easily led to accept Christ. But this person who has gone down into the depths of sin probably won't be saved right now."

Why not? If that moral, refined, beautiful girl takes Christ, God by His Holy Spirit will impart His nature to her and make her a child of God. But if the most immoral woman takes Christ, God by His Holy Spirit will impart His nature to her and make her His child in exactly the same way.

The most highly-educated, most upright, most attractive man will never be saved until the Holy Spirit makes him a new creation in Christ. The most hopeless, abandoned man can be born again and made a new creature the moment he accepts Christ.

We are all saved the same way—by the acceptance of Christ and the power of the Holy Spirit. Have you been born again? If not, will you receive Jesus right now and be born again?

Chapter 9

REFUGES OF LIES

"The hail shall sweep away the refuge of lies"—Isaiah 28:17.

Every one of us needs a refuge from four things—the accusations of our own conscience, the power of sin, the displeasure of God, and the wrath to come. The trouble is not that men have no refuge, but that they have a false one. Our text characterizes it as a refuge of lies.

God announces to us that there is a day coming for testing the refuges of men. In that day of testing, the hail will sweep away the refuge of lies. Is your refuge a true one or a false one? Is it a refuge that will stand the test of the hour that is coming, or is it a refuge that will go down in a day of storm?

There are four tests that you can apply to every hope that will show clearly whether it is a true hope or a refuge of lies. First, a true refuge must meet the highest demand of your conscience. If it is not a refuge from the accusations of your conscience, it is probably not a refuge from the displeasure of God. "For if our heart condemn us, God is greater than our heart, and knoweth all things" (1 John 3:20).

Second, trust in your refuge must make you a better person. If that refuge you trust is not making you a better person from day to day, it is not a refuge from the power of sin or from the wrath to come. Any hope that does not save you from the power of sin in this life can never save you from the consequences of sin in the life which is to come.

Third, it must stand the test of the dying hour. A refuge that only comforts you when you are well and strong, but fails when you are face to face with death, is absolutely worthless.

Finally, it must be a refuge that will stand the test of the Judgment Day. You may say you have a refuge that satisfies you. But will it satisfy God on Judgment Day? That's the question.

Our Own Righteousness

The first refuge of lies is trust in our own morality, our own goodness, or our own character. When you approach a person on the subject of becoming a Christian, he may reply, "No, I don't feel any need of Christ. I am trusting in my own character. Of course, I am not perfect, but I believe that the good in my life will more than make up for the evil. I am trusting in my own good deeds."

Let us apply our four tests. Does your goodness meet the highest demand of your conscience? In talking with highly moral people, I have met only two men who maintained that their own goodness came up to the highest demand of their conscience. You may think that they must have been remarkably good men. No, they had remarkably poor consciences.

I met one of these men when crossing the Atlantic Ocean. I started to talk to him one day about becoming a Christian, and he said to me, "I feel no need of a Savior."

I said, "Do you mean to tell me that you have never sinned?"

"Never," he said.

"Never fallen below the highest demand of your own conscience?"

"Never."

"Never done anything that you regretted afterward?"

"Never."

"Well," you say, "he must have been a good man indeed." Far from it. He was so mean that before we reached New York City, he was the most unpopular man on the ship.

Apply the second test: Is it trust in your own goodness making you a better person? As you go on talking about your own morality and trusting in it, do you find that you are growing more unselfish, more kind, more considerate of others, more helpful, and more humble? I have known a great many men who trusted in their own morality. Every one of them grew more cross, critical, self-centered, and proud.

Apply the third test: Will it stand the test of the dying hour? In days of health and strength a man will boast of his own goodness. But when he comes near death, he wishes that he had a living faith in Christ.

In one of my pastorates there was the most self-righteous man I ever knew. He had no use for the church, the Bible, Jesus Christ, and no use for ministers. He had a particular grudge against me because of something I had once done that he misunderstood. But he was perfectly confident that he was the best man in the community.

After many years, a cancer appeared on that man's scalp. It spread and ate its way through the scalp until it reached the skull. Little by little it ate its way through the skull until there was only a thin film of skull between the cancer and the brain. He knew he would soon die. In that hour he said, "Send for Mr. Torrey. I must speak to him."

I hurried to his home at once, sat down beside his bed, and he said, "Oh, Mr. Torrey, tell me how to be saved. Tell me how to become a Christian."

I took my Bible and I explained to him as simply as I knew how what to do to be saved. But somehow, he could not grasp it. Hour after hour I sat with him. When night came, I said to his wife and family, "You have sat up with him night after night. You go to bed, and I will sit up with him all night and minister to him." They gave me instructions what to do and retired for the night.

All night long I sat by him, except when I had to go into the other room to get something for him to eat or drink. Every time when I returned to the room where he was lying, there came a constant groan from his bed, "Oh, I wish I was a Christian!" And so the man died.

Will your own goodness stand the test of the Judgment Day? Someday you will stand face to face with God. That all-seeing, holy eye will look you through and through, the eye of the One who knows all your past, all your secret thoughts, and every hidden imagination. Will you look up into His face and say, "O God, Thou holy One, Thou all-seeing One, I stand here today confident that my own righteousness will satisfy Thee"? Never!

See if it will stand the test of the Word of God. We know that it will not. Paul warned us about trying to be saved by our own doings. "As many as are of the works of the law are under the curse: for it is written, Cursed is every one that continueth not in all things which are written in the book of the law to do them" (Galatians 3:10). We are told in Romans 3:20, "By the deeds of the law there shall no flesh living be justified in his sight."

Looking Good By Comparison

The second refuge of lies is trust in other people's badness. Some people make their boast in their own goodness; others make their boast in the badness of others. When you urge someone like this to come to Christ, he says, "No, I don't pretend to be very good, but I am just as good as a lot of other folks who are your church members."

Does it satisfy your conscience to say, "Well, I am not very good, but I am no worse than somebody else"? If it does, you must have an insensitive conscience. Is trust in other people's badness making you a better person? I have known many people who talked much of other people's badness, but I have yet to find anyone who was made better by the practice.

Show me a man who is always talking about the faults of others, and I will show you a man who is rotten at the heart. Show me a man that calls every other man a thief, and I will show you a man you can't trust with your wallet. Show me a man who thinks every other man is impure, and I will show you an adulterer. Show me a man or woman who is always talking about others' faults, and I will show you a man or woman that you can't trust. It never fails.

In one of my Bible classes I had a woman who was notoriously dishonest in business. One day she said to me, "Brother Torrey,"—she loved to use the word "brother"—"Brother Torrey, don't you think that everybody in business is dishonest?"

I looked at her and replied, "When anybody in business accuses everybody in business of being dishonest, they convict at least one person." She was furious! But why should she be? I only told her the truth.

Will you stand the test of the Judgment Day? Face to face with God who knows you, will you look up into His face and say, "I have never been good, but I am no worse than others"? Never! In that day, God tells us distinctly, "Every one of us shall give account of *himself* to God" (Romans 14:12).

God's Mercy And Judgment

The third refuge of lies is universalism—the belief that God is too good to condemn anyone, that there is no hell, and no future punishment for sin. How common a refuge that is today. When you urge people to come to Christ, they answer, "I believe in the mercy and goodness of God. I believe God is love and too good to condemn anyone. I don't believe in hell."

Does that satisfy the demands of your own conscience? When your conscience points out your sin and demands a change in your life, does it satisfy you to say, "Yes, I know my life is not right, but God is love; therefore, I am going right on trampling His laws underfoot, because He is so good and so loving." Is that the kind of conscience you have? Shame on you! Don't you ever do it again! God's infinite love gave His Son to die for you on the cross of Calvary.

Will your misinterpretation of God's goodness stand the test of the dying hour? A certain man

97

who was not a Christian became suddenly and seriously ill. His family saw that the illness might result in death, and they sent for their pastor. When he came into the room, this young fellow was tossing upon a bed of sickness. The pastor hurried to his side and tried to present to him the consolation of the gospel.

He said, "Pastor, I can't listen to you. I have heard it over and over again. I would not listen to it in times of health and strength. I am now very ill. I will die soon. I can't repent in my last hour."

His father paced the room in great anxiety. Finally, he said, "My son, there is nothing for you to be so anxious about. You have not been a bad boy, and there is no hell. You have nothing to fear."

His dying son turned to him and said, "Father, you have deceived me all through my life. If I had listened to Mother instead of to you, I would not be here now. She tried to get me to go to church and Sunday school, but you took me fishing instead. You told me that there was no hell, and I believed you. You have deceived me up to this time, but you can't deceive me any longer. I am dying and going to hell, and my blood is upon your soul." Then he turned his face to the wall and died.

Fathers, you who are undermining the teaching of godly wives, the day is coming when your sons will curse you. Will your universalism stand the test of the dying hour?

Is universalism making you a better man? Oh, with how many it is simply an excuse for sin! In many of our churches the world is sweeping in like a flood! All separation is gone, and professed Christians are running after the world, the flesh, and the devil. They have accepted the eternal hope nonsense which is robbing the Church of its devotion and beauty. The Church is becoming so like the world that you can't tell the two apart. Men have grown comfortable in a life of sin, giving up their separation to God.

Will it stand the test of the Judgment Day? When you meet God, will you look into His face and say, "O God, I know my life has not been right, but I thought that You were a God of love. I thought You were too good to punish sin. I did not think there was any hell, so I didn't bother to obey Your laws."

The Danger Of Unbelief

The next refuge of lies is infidelity. Let us apply the tests. Does your unbelief meet the highest demand of your own conscience? When conscience points out your sin and demands a new life, do you reply, "Well, I don't believe in the Bible, and I don't believe in God. I don't believe that Jesus Christ is the Son of God"? If that satisfies your conscience, you are not fit to be called a human being.

Is your unbelief making you a better man? My ministry has been largely a ministry to sceptics and agnostics. I have yet to meet the first unbeliever who was made better by his unbelief, but I have known many whose characters have been undermined by a lack of faith. I have had young men come to me with breaking hearts and with sad confessions of immorality and ruin. They tell me that the first step was listening to some ungodly lecturer or reading an ungodly book. Trifling with spiritual matters undermines the foundations of sound character. Unbelief is filling the world with wickedness.

In my own church in Chicago, to which a good many infidels come, one of them said to me, "We come over here to hear you. You don't spare us, but we like men who take a stand. That is the reason we come." There are always a lot of them every Sunday. Thank God, a great many of them get converted.

Will unbelief stand the test of the dying hour? How often it fails. A friend of mine who was in the army said that in the same company with him was a man who was a very outspoken unbeliever. On the second day of battle, he said to his fellow soldiers, "I have a strange feeling that I am going to be shot today."

"Nonsense," they said. "It is nothing but superstition. You are not going to be shot."

"Well," he said, "I feel very strange. I feel as if I am going to be shot."

At last they were lined up waiting for the word of command. "Forward, march!" They went up the hill, and just as they reached the summit, a volley came from the enemy's guns. A bullet pierced this man near the heart. He cried as they carried him to the rear, "O God, just give me time to repent." It only took one bullet to take the doubt out of that man. It should take less than that to take the nonsense out of you.

Will it stand the test of the Judgment Day? Will you go into God's presence and be ready to say, "God, my answer is this: I was an unbeliever; I was an agnostic; I was a sceptic; I was an atheist; I was a materialist." Do you think you will? Get down on your knees and try to tell Him. You can talk nonsense to your fellowmen. But when you talk to God, it will take the nonsense out of you.

Hiding Behind Religion

One more refuge of lies is religion. It may surprise you that religion is as much a refuge of lies as morality, other people's badness, universalim, or infidelity. Religion never saved anybody. It is one thing to trust in religion; it is something entirely different to trust in the living Christ.

You tell people about Christ, and they say, "Oh, I am very religious. I go to church. I say my prayers every morning and night. I read my Bible. I go to communion. I have been baptized. I have been confirmed. I give a tenth of my income to the poor. I am very religious." Well, you can do every bit of that and go straight to hell. Religion never saved anybody.

Is your religion making you a better man or woman? A great deal of religion will not make men or women one bit better. Many religious people will lie as fast as anybody. They will go around slandering their neighbors. Men who are prominent religious businessmen will cut you as wide open in a business deal as any man in town. They turn a deaf ear to the cry of the aged and the needy, unless it is going to get into the papers that they gave them something. Many men are very religious and are perfect scoundrels.

I met a man who seemed to be most religious. He made his employees gather together at a certain hour every day for prayer, and he held religious service with them every Sunday so that they would not have to go to church. But this pious hypocrite was paying the women that worked for him starvation wages. His employees were the palest, most sickly crowd of women I have ever seen. That kind of religion will send a man to the deepest part of hell.

Will your religion stand the test of the dying hour? A great many religious people are as badly scared as anybody when they come to die. I have heard them groan and sigh and weep in the dying hour. Their hollow religion doesn't stand the test of great crisis.

Will it stand the test of the Judgment Day? The Lord Jesus Christ says, "Many will say to me in that day, Lord, Lord, have we not prophesied in thy name? and in thy name have cast out devils? and in thy name done many wonderful works? And then will I profess unto them, I never knew you: depart from me, ye that work iniquity" (Matthew 7:22-23). Religion is a refuge of lies, and if that is what you are trusting in, you will be lost forever.

The Sure Foundation

Is there no true refuge? Yes, there is. God says, "Behold, I lay in Zion for a foundation a stone, a tried stone, a precious cornerstone, a sure foundation: he that believeth shall not make haste" (Isaiah 28:16).

That sure foundation stone is Jesus Christ. "Other foundation can no man lay than that is laid, which is Jesus Christ" (1 Corinthians 3:11). It is one thing to trust in religion and something entirely different to trust in a crucified and risen Christ with a living faith.

Will that refuge stand the test of our own conscience? When my conscience points to my sin, I have an answer that satisfies it. Jesus bore my sins on the cross. Will it make men better men? Yes. A living faith in a crucified and living Christ will make every man who has it more like Christ every day. If you have a faith that is not making you like Christ, you do not have a real faith.

Will it stand the test of the Judgment Day? Yes. If it is God's will, I am willing to face Him tonight in judgment. You say, "What! Have you never sinned?" Certainly I have. You will never know how deeply I have sinned. But when God asks for

103

an answer, I will say one word—"Jesus"—and that will satisfy God.

The hail shall sweep away every refuge of lies. Throw them all away and come to Christ. Be ready for life, ready for death, and ready for eternity.

Chapter 10

FOUND OUT

Every sin has a consequense
if not now for eternity
A) Talk about how we pay here
B) Talk about payment in eternity
no one skies out
no one get by w/anything
no one fools God

"Be sure your sin will find you out"—Numbers 32:23.

No man can escape his sins. Every sin we commit will find us out, call us to account, and make us pay. No man ever committed a sin that he did not pay for in some way. The most serious folly of which a man can be guilty is for him to imagine that he can ever gain anything by doing wrong. Whether you hurt anyone else by your own wrongdoing or not, you are sure to hurt yourself.

If a man puts his hand in the fire, he will be burned. If a man sins, he will certainly suffer for each sin he commits. You may escape the laws of men, but you cannot escape the law of God. No man can hide where his sin will not find him.

Men's sins find them out by *the execution of human laws*. The execution of law in society is necessarily imperfect, and yet, it is astonishing how often men who break the laws are sooner or later punished for their crime. A man may success-

Consequences

fully elude the meshes of the law for months or even years, but he is all the time weaving a net that will almost certainly entrap him at last. It is a marvelous thing how crime comes to light. A man's sin finds him out and exposes him at last to the contempt of the whole world.

Men's sins find them out *in their own bodies.* When a man does not pay the penalty of his sin in human courts, he pays it in a court where there is no possibility of bribery—the court of physical retribution for moral offenses. In a general way, there is an intimate connection between morality and health. All sins have physical consequences. The consequences of some sins are often not immediate or definitely traceable to specific sins, but it remains true that every sin has some physical consequences.

Young men see others suffering the terrible consequences of transgressing God's law, yet they go right on as an ox to the slaughter. They suppose that they will be an exception. There are no exceptions to physical law. Any action that is unnatural or immoral is bound to be visited with penalty. Why are there so many men with broken bodies and shattered intellects? Why so many broken-down women? The answer is the violation of God's law—their sins are finding them out.

Of course, disease may be hereditary or the result of accident or misfortune. But if we should eliminate all the sickness that is the direct or indi-

if everyone thinks they will be the exception, there are no exceptions. God sees & knows all, we get away w/ nothing

rect result of our own sin, we would be surprised at the relatively small amount of sickness left.

Consider a sin such as anger. Does it affect a man's body? It causes disorders in his blood, stomach, brain, and nerves. It is obviously unhealthy in every case and may even lead to paralysis and death. It is amazing the many ways, some direct and some indirect, in which our sins find us out in our own bodies. If you are contemplating sin, just stop and think of this—Be sure your sin will find you out!

Damaging To Character And Conscience ③

For every sin you commit, *you will suffer in character*. Sin breeds a moral ulcer. A diseased character is worse than a diseased body. You can't tell a lie without your moral blood being poisoned by it and your moral health undermined.

Do you think you can cheat a man in business and not suffer in your character more than he suffers in his pocket? Do you think you can wrong an employee in his wages and not suffer more in what you become than he suffers in what he gets? Do you think you can wrong a man regarding his wife and not have a deadly cancer develop in your own character? Do you think you can read an impure book or listen to an obscene story and not breed a stinking corruption in your own moral nature? Do you think you can violate those laws of purity that God has written in His Word and on your heart and not reap the consequences in your own character?

The reaping of sin is a ghastly business. a lifetime of responsibility for a night of passion. The losing a friend for 1 careless word sometimes we pay 100 & 1000 fold

Sin always finds people out in their characters, in what they become.

Again, your sin will find you out in *your own conscience.* You can hide your sin from everyone but yourself. You are so constructed by God that to know you are a sinner means self-condemnation and agony. Many suffer from the bitter consciousness of sins that no one else knows anything about. No physical torments can match the torments of an accusing conscience. An accusing conscience means hell on earth. No earthly prosperity, no human love, no mirth, music, fun, or intoxication can dispel its clouds or assuage the agony of its gnawing tooth. That sin you are contemplating looks fair and sweet. It won't look so fair or taste so sweet after it is committed. It will find you out, and you will suffer.

Your sin will find you out *in the lives of your children.* One of the most awful things about sin is that its curse falls not only upon us, but upon our children also. You may complain about that as much as you like, but it is an unquestionable fact.

I remember a man who was a constant, but moderate drinker. He had three sons. I don't think that man was ever drunk in his life. He despised a drunkard, but he laughed at total abstainers. Each one of his three sons became alcoholics. A wise friend of mine says he never has known a man in the liquor business where the curse sooner or later did not strike his own home.

Facing Eternity

There is one more place where your sin will find you out—your sin will find you out *in eternity*. This present life is not all that there is. Our acts and their consequences will follow us into our future life. If your sin does not find you out here, it will there. You may be absolutely sure of that. In eternity we will reap the consequences of every sin we sowed here on earth.

Life sometimes seems to go on here to the end without justice. Men defraud their employees, they rob the needy, they condemn other men and their families to poverty, that they may increase their already enormous wealth. No one seems to call them to account. It will not always be so. God will call them to strict account. A few thousands or millions of their ill-gotten wealth given to charity will not blind the eyes of a holy God. They will suffer.

Men sometimes lay traps for foolish girls, causing them to ruin their reputations. Yet, no one seems to call the man to account. He goes on, accepted in the "best society," and is loaded with honors. His sin will find him out, however, if not in this world, in the next. He will stand before the universe exposed to shame, loaded with dishonor, cast out to everlasting contempt.

Men despise God, laugh at His Word, and trample underfoot His Son, yet God still lets them live. He does not seem to call them to account. But it will not be always so. "Be sure your sin will find you out."

"The Lord Jesus shall be revealed from heaven with his mighty angels, in flaming fire taking vengeance on them that know not God, and that obey not the Gospel of our Lord Jesus Christ: who shall be punished with everlasting destruction from the presence of the Lord, and from the glory of his power" (2 Thessalonians 1:7-9).

You cannot sin without suffering for it. Your sin will find you out in the court of law, in your own body, in your character, in your conscience, in your children, in eternity, or in all of these put together. You will suffer. You will pay an awful price. Your sin will find you out.

But many of us have sinned already, and our sins are finding us out now. What shall we do? There is only one way of escape from the penalties of the law—the grace of the gospel. "Christ has redeemed us from the curse of the law, being made a curse for us" (Galatians 3:13). He calls, "Come unto me, all ye that labour and are heavy laden, and I will give you rest" (Matthew 11:28).

1st half of great
sermon
finish by talking
about forgiveness

Chapter 11

SALVATION IS FOR YOU

"Who then can be saved?"—Mark 10:26.

The disciples asked Jesus that question. Jesus had just told them how hard it was for a rich man to enter into the Kingdom of heaven. The disciples seem to have held the same opinion that most men do today—a rich man can get anywhere. But Jesus said that it was easier for a camel to pass through the eye of a needle than for a rich man to enter the Kingdom of God.

Who then can be saved? Jesus went on to tell them that although it was impossible through man's power for a rich man to be saved, God, with whom all things are possible, could save even a rich man. But only God could.

We come, then, to the question itself: "Who then can be saved?" The Bible answers the question clearly. The Bible tells us that there are some people who cannot be saved, and that there are some people who can be saved.

> no one can be saved it is impossible even for the 111 cream of society to get close to God on their own merit

Who Cannot Be Saved?

1) *No man can be saved who will not give up his sin.* We read in Isaiah 55:7, "Let the wicked forsake his way, and the unrighteous man his thoughts: and let him return unto the Lord; and he will have mercy upon him; and to our God, for he will abundantly pardon."

Every man and woman has to choose between sin and salvation. You cannot have both. If you won't give up sin, you must give up salvation. Absurd schemes of salvation propose to save a man while he continues in sin. We read in Matthew 1:21 concerning our Savior, "Thou shalt call his name JESUS: for he shall save his people *from* their sins." Sin is damnation; holiness is salvation.

The reason why some people are not saved is because they don't want to give up sin. Some won't give up drunkenness or adultery or profanity or lying or their bad temper. You cannot be saved if you want to sin. If you persist in sinning, you will be lost forever.

2) *No man can be saved who trusts in his own righteousness and is not willing to admit that he is a lost sinner.* Thousands of lost sinners are proud of their own morality. They are not willing to get down to the dust and say, "I am a poor, vile, worthless, miserable sinner." You can never be saved while you trust in your own righteousness.

Jesus tells us that two men went up to the temple to pray. One was a Pharisee, one of the most

112

respectable religious men in the community. The other was a publican, a man whom everybody looked down upon. The Pharisee talked about his own goodness when he prayed. He looked up and said, "I thank Thee, O God, that I am not as other men are—unjust, extortioners, adulterers." He looked contemptuously over to the poor publican, "Or even as this publican. I fast twice every week. I give a tenth of all I get." Jesus said that this man went out of the temple an unforgiven, hopelessly lost sinner.

But the publican, the outcast, the man that everybody looked down upon, would not so much as lift up his eyes to heaven. He felt he was a miserable, worthless sinner. He beat his breast and said, "God be merciful to me a sinner!" Jesus said that this man went down to his house justified. (See Luke 18:10-14.) Anybody can be saved that will take the sinner's place and cry for mercy.

The World's Largest Family

One day a friend of mine, an old Scotchman, was walking through the country when a man came along and stopped beside him. The man started up a conversation with the old Scotchman, curious about his background. My friend said, "I will tell you who I am, and I will tell you what my business is. I have a very strange business. I am hunting for heirs."

The other man said, "What?"

"I am hunting for heirs to a great estate. I

113

represent a very great estate, and I am hunting for heirs for it. There are a good many in this neighborhood."

The other said, "Do you mind telling me their names?"

"No," he said. "It is a very large family. Their name begins with 'S.' "

"Oh," said the man. "Smith, I suppose?"

"No," the old man replied, "a much larger family than the Smith family."

"Larger than the Smith family! Who are they?"

The old Scotchman said, "They are the sinner family. The estate I represent is the Kingdom of God, the inheritance is incorruptible, undefiled, and does not fade away. The heirs to it are the sinners who are willing to take the family name, admit that they are sinners, and look to God for pardon." *Good illustration*

Do you belong to the sinner family? If you do, you can be saved. If you are not willing to admit that you do, you cannot be saved. You are lost forever.

No *man or woman can be saved who is not willing to accept salvation as a free gift.* We are told in Ephesians 2:8, "For by grace are ye saved through faith; and that not of yourselves: it is the gift of God." "The gift of God is eternal life through Jesus Christ our Lord" (Romans 6:23). Salvation is a free gift. Anybody can have it for nothing; nobody can have it any other way. If you are not willing to take it as a free gift, you cannot have it at all.

My wife was talking to a young man, a son of the richest man in the neighborhood. There seemed to be some difficulty about his accepting Christ. Finally my wife said to him, "The trouble with you is you are not willing to accept salvation as a free gift."

"Mrs. Torrey, that is just it. I am not willing to accept salvation as a free gift. If I could earn it, if I could work for it, if I could deserve it, then it would be different. I am willing to earn it, but I am not willing to take it as a free gift."

Nobody can earn it; nobody can merit it; nobody can deserve it. Unless you are willing to take it as a free gift, you will never get it at all. The richest man on earth that gets saved will have nothing more to boast about when he gets to heaven than the lowliest beggar who is saved.

Sincerely Wrong

4) *Nobody can be saved who will not accept Jesus Christ as his Savior.* "There is none other name under heaven given among men, whereby we must be saved" (Acts 4:12). Anybody can be saved in Christ; nobody can be saved in any other way. An infidel once said to a friend of mine, "If I cannot be saved without accepting Christ, I won't be saved." Well, then, he won't be saved. That is all there is to it.

If you ever go to Sydney, Australia, you will soon

find that every citizen in that city is very proud of their harbor. You won't be in Sydney long before somebody will ask you, "What do you think of our harbor?" They should be proud of it. It is one of the finest harbors in the world. But it has only one entrance. There is one enormous rock called the North Head, and another called the South Head. The only channel, wide and deep, is between these two heads. A little way south of the South Head is another headland, called Jacob's Ladder.

One night, many years ago, a vessel called the *Duncan Dunbar,* with hundreds of people on board, came outside of Sydney harbor after dark. The captain saw the South Head and thought it was the North Head. He saw Jacob's Ladder and thought it was the South Head. He steered, put on full speed, steamed in between the two lights, and ran onto the rocks. Every one of the hundreds on board perished, except one man who was thrown up into a cave on the face of the rock.

That captain was perfectly sincere—there never was a more sincere man on earth—but he was mistaken, and he was lost. People say it does not make any difference what you believe if you are only sincere. But the more sincerely you believe error, the worse off you are. There is just one channel into salvation, and that is Christ. Try to go any other way, no matter how sincere you are, and you will be wrecked and lost eternally.

116

Who Can Be Saved?

Sinners can be saved, even the most depraved.
"This is a faithful saying, and worthy of all acceptation, that Christ Jesus came into the world to save sinners; of whom I am chief" (1 Timothy 1:15). He has already saved the chief of sinners, and He is able to do it again. *worst one, how was saved*

In the city where I used to live, a young girl of thirteen became pregnant. Her father and mother disowned her. Her brothers rejected her, and I doubt if they were any better than she was. They cast this poor girl of only thirteen years of age into the streets to fend for herself. She soon became the companion of thieves, robbers, murderers, of everything that was disreputable. She lost the baby because of her poor health and became a member of two of the worst gangs, at different times, in New York and Chicago.

A friend of mine met her one night and said, "If you are ever sick of this life, come to me, and I will help you out of it." A time came when she was thoroughly sick of it, and she went to this gentleman's house. He was a very wealthy man, who used all his money for God. He showed her the way of life, and she was saved. That young woman went on to occupy a high position of great responsibility and honor in her city. There is scarcely anyone who even knows her past life. God has covered it up, though she still has the same name.

A few years ago I was in her town. She came to me and said, "I hope, Mr. Torrey, that you won't think it necessary to tell the people here my story." My wife and I were the only ones there that knew her past record. She had been in our house in the days of her trouble.

I said, "Most assuredly we shall not." Why should you tell a saved woman's story, when it is underneath the blood of Jesus? It is no longer her story. It is blotted out. Jesus Christ not only saved her out of the depths of sin, but He covered up her past as well.

Depending On His Power

Any man or woman who is too weak to resist sin in their own strength can be saved. It is not a question of your strength, but of Christ's strength. "Now unto him that is able to keep you from falling, and to present you faultless before the presence of his glory with exceeding joy" (Jude 24). "Who are kept by the power of God through faith unto salvation" (1 Peter 1:5). Jesus Christ can keep the weakest man or woman just as well as the strongest. Why because Christs power now

I have seen men start out in the Christian life who talk this way in testimony meetings: "Friends, you know me; I am a man with great strength of character. When I make up my mind to do anything, I always follow through. I have started out in this Christian life, and I want you to understand that I am not going to backslide as so many do. I

118

am going through." Whenever I hear a man talking that way, I know he is going to backslide within six weeks.

Another man will stand up trembling, hesitant, and he will say, "You all know me. You know I have no will power left. I have tried to quit my sin time and time again. As you know, I have failed every time. I have absolutely no confidence in myself. But God says in Isaiah 41:10, 'Fear thou not; for I am with thee: be not dismayed; for I am thy God: I will strengthen thee; yea, I will help thee; yea, I will uphold thee with the right hand of my righteousness.' I am trusting in Him." When I hear a man talking that way, I know he is going to stand every time.

One day somebody came to me in Chicago and said, "We have got to find a place for this woman to stay. Her husband got drunk last night and tried to kill her with a knife. It is not safe for her or her child, so she has left him. We must do something to provide for her."

I said, "You are right to provide for her; that is just what we should do."

A few days later, her husband came to me and said, "Mr. Torrey, do you know where my wife is?"

I said, "I do."

"Will you please tell me where she is?"

"I will not. You tried to kill her. You do not deserve to have a wife. I am not going to tell you where she is so that you may go and kill her."

He said, "If you do not tell me, I will commit suicide."

"Very well," I said. "You will go to hell if you do." A man like him never commits suicide. He kept getting drunk instead. He could not help it, poor fellow. Every now and then, he would come to me for a few dollars, saying that he was going to get a job in a shoe factory. I always knew that the money was going for whiskey. He was always saying that he was going to quit drinking. I knew he was not. He meant to. He would say that he was hunting for work. But I knew he was looking for another drink.

That went on for years. One day I said to God, "Heavenly Father, if you will give me this man, I will never despair of the salvation of another man as long as I live." Very soon afterward, he got his feet upon the Rock, Christ Jesus, and never fell again.

Years passed, and he became an honored member of my church. When I returned for a visit, among those who came to welcome me was this man, his wife, and a child, a happy family in Jesus Christ. The Christ who saved the lying, habitual, hopeless drunkard can save anyone that will trust Him.

Power For Deliverance

Any man can be saved who thinks he has committed the unpardonable sin, if he is willing to come to Jesus Christ. Jesus says in John 6:37,

"Him that cometh to me I will in no wise cast out." I think I have never gone anywhere in my life where somebody has not said, "I have committed the unpardonable sin." Almost every one, if not every one, has gone away rejoicing in Jesus.

One time I received a brokenhearted letter from a father who was a Presbyterian minister. He wrote that he had a son who was in deep spiritual darkness. The son thought that he had committed the unpardonable sin, and he was plunged into absolute despair. Would I take him into the Bible Institute? I replied that though I had every sympathy for him in his sorrow, the Bible Institute was not for the purpose of helping cases like these but to train men and women for Christian service.

The father continued to write, begging me to take his son, and he got other friends to plead for him. Finally, I consented to take the young man. He was sent to me under guard, to prevent him from doing something rash on the way.

When he was brought to my office, I showed him to a seat. As soon as the others had left the room, he began the conversation by saying, "I am possessed of the devil."

"I think quite likely you are," I replied, "but Christ is able to cast out devils."

"You do not understand me," he said. "I mean that the devil has entered into me as he did into Judas Iscariot."

"That may be," I answered, "but Christ came to destroy the works of the devil. He says in John

6:37, 'Him that cometh to me I will in no wise cast out.' If you will just come to Him, He will receive you and set you free from Satan's power."

The conversation went on in this way for some time. He constantly asserted the absolute hopelessness of his case, and I constantly claimed the power of Jesus Christ and His promise, "Him that cometh to me I will in no wise cast out."

Days and weeks passed, and we had many conversations, always on the same line. One day I met him in the hall of the Institute and made up my mind that the time had come to have the battle out. I invited him to my office and told him to sit down. "Do you believe the Bible?" I asked.

"Yes," he replied, "I believe everything in it."

"Do you believe that Jesus Christ told the truth when He said, 'Him that cometh to me I will in no wise cast out?' "

"Yes, I do. I believe everything in the Bible."

"Well, then, will you come to Christ?"

"I have committed the unpardonable sin."

I replied, "Jesus does not say, 'Him that hath not committed the unpardonable sin that cometh to me I will in no wise cast out.' He says, 'Him that cometh to me I will in no wise cast out.' "

"But I have sinned willfully after I have received the knowledge of the truth."

"Jesus does not say, 'Him that has not sinned willfully after he received the knowledge of the truth that cometh unto me I will in no wise cast out.' He says, 'Him that cometh to me I will in no wise cast out,' " I said.

"But I have been enlightened and tasted the heavenly gift and have fallen away. It is impossible to renew me again unto repentance."

"Jesus does not say, 'Him that has not tasted of the heavenly gift, and has not fallen away, if he cometh to me I will in no wise cast him out.' He says, 'Him that cometh to me I will in no wise cast out.' "

He continued with his excuses. "But I am possessed of the devil. The devil has entered into me as he did into Judas Iscariot. My heart is hard as a millstone."

I answered every one of his protests with the same scripture, John 6:37, until his excuses were exhausted. I looked him square in the face and said, "Now, will you come? Get down on your knees, and quit your nonsense." He knelt, and I knelt by his side. "Now," I said, "follow me in prayer."

"Lord Jesus," I said, and he repeated, "Lord Jesus. My heart is as hard as a millstone. I have no desire to come to You. But You said in Your Word, 'Him that cometh to me I will in no wise cast out.' I believe this statement of Yours. Therefore, though I don't feel it, I believe You have received me."

When he had finished, I said, "Did you really come?"

He replied, "I did."

"Has He received you?"

"I do not feel it," he replied.

"But what does He say?"

"Him that cometh to me I will in no wise cast out."

"Is this true? Does Jesus tell the truth, or does He lie?"

"He tells the truth."

"What, then, must He have done?"

"He must have received me."

"Now," I said, "go to your room. Stand firmly upon this promise of Jesus Christ. The devil will give you an awful conflict, but just answer him every time with John 6:37. Stand right there, believing what Jesus says in spite of your feelings, in spite of what the devil may say, in spite of everything."

He went to his room. The devil did give him an awful conflict, but he stood firmly on John 6:37 and came out of his room triumphant and radiant.

Years have passed since then. Though the devil tried again and again to plunge him into despair, he stood firmly on John 6:37. He was used of God to do larger work for Christ than almost any man I know. He is the author of that hymn,

"Years I spent in vanity and pride,
Caring not my Lord was crucified,
Knowing not it was for me He died
On Calvary.

"Mercy there was great, and grace was free,
Pardon there was multiplied to me,

Great Story

Track down author to this hymn.

124

There my burdened soul found liberty,
At Calvary."

Anyone can be saved that will come to Jesus. "The Spirit and the bride say, Come. And let him that heareth say, Come. And let him that is athirst come. And whosoever will, let him take the water of life freely" (Revelation 22:17).

Chapter 12

HOW TO FIND REST

"Come unto me, all ye that labour and are heavy laden, and I will give you rest. Take my yoke upon you, and learn of me; for I am meek and lowly in heart: and ye shall find rest unto your souls"——Matthew 11:28-29.

What this world needs is rest. What every man and woman who is not already in Christ needs is rest. Millions of people work hard for small pay and go home night after night to wretched homes, worn out, without any fit place to sleep. Millions more have no rest for their heart, no rest for their souls.

There is One who can give rest to every tired heart. His name is Jesus Christ. He stands with extended hands and says, "Come unto me, all ye that labour and are heavy laden, and I will give you rest."

Those are either the words of a divine Being or the words of a lunatic. If the Lord Jesus Christ offers rest and gives it, He is a divine Being. If He offers rest and cannot give it, He is a lunatic. If any man, even the greatest and the best that the world ever saw, held out his hands to this sorrowing, grief-stricken, burdened world of ours and said, "Come unto me, and I will give you rest," you would know at once that the man had gone crazy, for no man could do it. But Jesus offers to do it, and He does it. Millions throughout the centuries have accepted Christ's offer. Nobody who ever accepted it failed to find rest.

Whom Did Jesus Call?

There was a great throng when the Lord Jesus spoke that day. That crowd represented lives filled with misery. There were multitudes of the poor there, the penniless, the sick, the demonic, and the outcast—a vast mass of misery. The Lord Jesus Christ cast His loving eye over that great multitude that represented so much misery, and His great heart went out to them. He said, "Come, come to Me, every one of you who has a burden, every one who has a sorrow, every one who has a broken heart. Come to Me, and I will give you rest."

He extends His hands to all men and all women in all ages that are burdened, down-trodden, oppressed, wretched, brokenhearted, and filled with despair. He invited all that labor and are heavy laden.

Some commentators have tried to tone down the words of our Lord. They tell us that He meant all who were burdened with the many requirements of the Mosaic law. Others tell us He meant all who were burdened by a consciousness of sin, a sense of guilt. Jesus means just what He says. "Come unto me, *all* ye that labour"—every man that has a burden, a sorrow, a heartache, a trouble, a woe of any kind—Jesus invites you to come.

He invites all who are burdened with a sense of sin and shame. Perhaps you feel that your life is disgraceful. You are ashamed of yourself, and you hardly lift up your head. You are saying to yourself, "My life is simply shameful," and you are crushed by the sense of your sin. Jesus says to you, "Come unto me, and I will give you rest."

A Woman Transformed

That day when our Lord Jesus spoke these words in Capernaum, on the outskirts of the crowd, was a woman who was a prostitute, an outcast despised by everyone. As she stood there, I have no doubt many women who prided themselves on their morality turned and looked at her with scorn. But soon Jesus looked at her too—not with scorn, but with pity, with compassion, with tenderness, with yearning, with love. She saw He was speaking directly to her. He seemed to lose sight of everybody else as He stretched His hands out toward her and said, "Come unto me, all ye that labour and are heavy laden, and I will give you rest."

That woman said in amazement, "He means me." When the crowd broke up, she followed at a distance to see where Jesus went. Jesus went to the house of Simon, the Pharisee, who had invited Him to dinner. She hurried to her home, took a very costly box of ointment, the most expensive thing that she had, and hurried back to Simon's house. As Jesus reclined there in the Oriental way, she came up behind Him, bent over His feet, and began to bathe them with her tears.

The other guests looked up in scorn. They grumbled. "This man pretends to be a prophet. He is no prophet, or He would not allow that woman to touch Him. If He were a prophet, He would know what kind of a woman she is. She is a sinner."

Well, He did know. He knew better than any of them did, not only that she was a sinner, but that she was a repenting sinner. While His feet were still wet with her tears, she wiped them with the long tresses of her beautiful hair. Then she broke over them the alabaster box of precious ointment. The Lord Jesus turned to her and said, "Woman, your sins are all forgiven." Then He said again, "Woman, your faith has saved you. Go in peace." That woman, who stood on the outskirts of that crowd with a breaking heart, left that house with the peace of God in her soul. (See Luke 7:36-50.)

Freedom From Bondage

The Lord Jesus invites every man and woman who is burdened by the bondage of sin. There are some of you who are in bondage to alcohol. You want to be sober and to lead an upright life. You have tried again and again to give up drinking but have failed. Others are burdened with the desire for drugs. You have tried to be free from your bondage. The Lord Jesus says to you, "Come unto me and I will give you rest."

You may be burdened with impurity or some disgusting sin. You have tried to break away time and time again, until at last you have given up. You are utterly discouraged, crushed by the power of your sin. If you could read the secret sorrow of every heart, you would find hundreds of people crushed to the earth by the power of sin. The Lord Jesus says to everyone, "Come unto me all ye that labour and are heavy laden, and I will give you rest."

I have a dear friend who was carefully reared by a godly mother. His father had been an alcoholic. His mother was afraid that her son would become a drunkard, so she made him promise that he would never touch a drop of liquor. He lived for eighteen years without tasting it.

One day he was on a business trip with a friend. On the way back the man bought some alcohol and asked him to have a drink. "No," he said, "I promised my mother never to drink."

"Well," he said, "if you don't drink you will insult me." That elderly man worked on that boy until he got him to drink his first glass of whiskey. It was as though a demon in him was set on fire. From that time on, he became a drunkard. He lost one job after another, and at last was a wrecked man in New York City. He wrote one hundred and thirty-eight bad checks against his last employer, and the officers of the law were looking for him.

One awful night, he went into a bar and for a long time sat there in a drunken stupor. He suddenly began to feel all the horrors of delirium tremors coming over him. He thought he was going to die. He went up to the bar and ordered a drink. Then he threw down the glass and said, "Men, hear me, hear me; I shall never drink another glass of whiskey, even if it kills me."

They all laughed at him. He went out of the bar and down to the police station. He said to the sergeant at the desk, "Lock me up; I am going to have the tremors; lock me up!" The sergeant took him down to the cell and locked him up.

He spent a night and a day in awful agony. The next evening, somebody said to him, "Why don't you go to the city mission?" In an awful condition, he went down to the mission and listened to one man after another give his testimony of how he was saved. When the minister asked all who wanted to receive Christ to come to the front, he went up to the front, knelt down, and said, "Pray for me."

The minister responded, "Pray for yourself."

"Oh," he said, "I don't know how to pray. I have forgotten how to pray."

The minister softly repeated, "Pray for yourself." That wrecked and ruined man lifted up his broken heart to Jesus. Jesus met him and took the bondage of alcohol from him that same night. That man became one of the most respected men in New York City.

Are you burdened? Have you fought against sin and failed? Have you tried again and again, perhaps signed pledge after pledge, only to break it? Are you burdened with the weight of an overcoming sin? Jesus holds out His hand to you. He says, "Come unto me all ye that labour and are heavy laden, and I will give you rest."

There is a cure for every sorrow at the feet of Jesus. I have a beautiful family Bible which my mother gave to my grandmother at the time of my grandfather's death. On the flyleaf of the Bible in my mother's own beautiful handwriting are these words, "Earth hath no sorrow that heaven cannot heal." That is true, but something better is true. Earth has no sorrow that Jesus cannot heal right now, before we get to heaven.

Lifting The Burden Of Doubt

The Lord Jesus invites all who are burdened by doubt and unbelief. To some men, doubt and unbelief are not a burden. They are glad that they are sceptics. They are proud of their doubts. But to a man of any real moral earnestness, doubt is a burden, a heavy load—he is never proud of doubt. An earnest-minded man wants truth, not uncertainty, and knowledge of God to replace agnosticism.

There are some who honestly doubt, and their doubt is a burden. Jesus says, "Come unto me all ye that are burdened with doubt, and I will give you rest."

Am I suggesting that a sceptic come to Christ, an unbeliever come to Christ, an agnostic come to Christ? Certainly; He is the best One you can come to.

Thomas was a sceptic. The other disciples had seen our Lord after His resurrection. Thomas was not present. When Thomas came back, the other disciples said, "We have seen the Lord." He said, "I don't believe it. I don't believe you have seen the Lord, and I won't believe it unless I see Him with my own eyes, put my fingers into the prints of the nails in His hands, and thrust my hand into His side."

But Thomas was an honest doubter. When he thought that perhaps the Lord Jesus would be around the next Sunday evening, he was there. He came to Jesus with his doubts. Jesus scattered every one of them, and Thomas cried, "My Lord and my God." (See John 20:24-28.)

Nathaniel was an honest doubter and a thorough sceptic. Philip came to him and said, "Nathaniel, we have found Him of whom Moses in the law, and the prophets, wrote—Jesus of Nazareth, the son of Joseph."

Nathaniel said, "I don't believe He is the Messiah. He came from Nazareth. Can any good thing come out of Nazareth?"

Philip said, "You come and see." That is the thing to do—come and see. Nathaniel said, "I will

133

come." He came along with Philip. He met the Lord, and he had not been with the Lord ten minutes when all his doubts were gone. Nathaniel cried, "You are the Son of God, the King of Israel." (See John 1:45-49.)

If you are burdened with doubt, bring your doubts to Jesus. Whatever your burden is, Jesus invites you, every burdened one, every heavy-hearted one, to come to Him.

Come Only To Jesus

Jesus says, "Come unto *Me*"—not, "Come unto the church." The church cannot give you rest. I believe in the church; I believe every converted man should be a member of some church, but the church never gave anybody rest. The church is full of people who have never found rest. They have come to the church instead of coming to Jesus Himself.

Jesus does not say, "Come to a creed." I believe in creeds. I think every man ought to have a creed. A creed is simply an intelligent, systematic statement of what a man believes. A man should believe something and be able to state intelligently what he believes. If he is an intelligent, studious man, his creed will be getting longer all the time. But there was never a creed written or printed that would give anybody rest. It is not going to a creed; it is going to the personal Savior.

The Lord Jesus does not say, "Come unto the priest" or "Come unto the preacher" or "Come unto the evangelist" or "Come unto any other man." He says, "Come unto Me." No preacher can give you rest; no priest can give you rest; no man can give you rest. Jesus says, "Come unto Me."

I have sometimes asked people if they have come to Jesus, and they say, "Oh, I am a Protestant." Well, that never saved anybody. There will be lots of Protestants in hell. Others say, "I am a Roman Catholic." That never saved anybody either. There will be lots of Roman Catholics in hell. When a man says, "I am a Roman Catholic," I say, "I am not asking you that. Have you come to Jesus?" It is not a question of whether you are a Roman Catholic or a Protestant. Have you come to Jesus? If you have not, will you come now?

Come to Jesus, take His yoke, surrender absolutely to Him; commit all your sins to Him to pardon; commit all your doubts to Him to remove; commit all your thoughts to Him to teach; commit yourself to believe in Him, to learn from Him, to obey Him, to serve Him. The moment you come to Him with all your heart and cast yourself upon Him, He will give you rest. You can have rest right now.

One night in my church in Chicago, one of the officers of my church went to the upper balcony after I was through preaching. He stepped up to a gentleman and said, "Are you saved?"

"Yes, sir," he said, "I am saved." He was very positive about it.

"How long have you been saved?"

He said, "About five minutes."

"When were you saved?"

He motioned toward the platform and said, "While that man was preaching." He did not wait until I finished my sermon. He came to Jesus right then, and Jesus saved him right there.

Will you come? Lose sight of everyone else, and see the Lord Jesus standing there, holding out His hands to you with a heart bursting with love, breaking with pity and compassion. He says to every heavy-hearted man and woman, "Come unto me all ye that labour and are heavy laden, and I will give you rest." Will you come?

Chapter 13

JOY UNSPEAKABLE

"Though now ye see him not, yet believing, ye rejoice with joy unspeakable and full of glory"—1 Peter 1:8.

Christians are the happiest people in the world. According to our text they "rejoice with joy unspeakable and full of glory," and nobody else does. Why are Christians so happy?

First of all, *Christians are happy because they know that their sins are all forgiven.* "All that believe are justified from all things" (Acts 13:39). Christians know their sins are forgiven because the Holy Spirit bears witness of forgiveness in their hearts.

The apostle Peter preached about Jesus in the household of Cornelius. He said, "To him give all the prophets witness, that through his name whosoever believeth in him shall receive remission of sins" (Acts 10:43). Cornelius and his whole household believed it, and immediately, the Spirit of God came upon them.

When you and I believe in Jesus, His Spirit comes into our hearts, bearing witness with our spirit that our sins are all forgiven and that we are children of God. There is no joy on earth like the joy of knowing that God has forgiven and blotted out every sin you ever committed.

Suppose a person was in prison for some crime, and someone brought him a pardon—don't you think he would be happy? But that is nothing compared to knowing that God has forgiven all your sins. Oh, the joy that comes into the heart when a man knows that every sin he ever committed is blotted out, and that God has absolutely nothing against him.

A great king wrote a song of joy that has lived through the centuries. That king had been a great sinner, and God had forgiven his sin. He had much to be happy about. He was the greatest king of his day. He had great wealth and great armies. He was the greatest general of the time, and he had a great palace. But when he wrote his song of joy he did not say, "Happy is the man that has a beautiful palace" or "Happy is the man that has great armies" or "Happy is the man that is loved by his people." He said, "Blessed is he whose transgression is forgiven, whose sin is covered. Blessed is the man unto whom the Lord imputeth not iniquity, and in whose spirit there is no guile" (Psalm 32:1-2). Every man who receives the Lord Jesus as his Savior will have his sins forgiven and will have the joy of knowing that every sin is blotted out.

Sons Of The King

Christians are happy because they are set free from sin's power. Everybody who sins is a slave to sin. Since ancient times, many nations and races have been subject to the harshness of slavery. Some of the masters were kind and some were cruel. But there was never a slave-owner that was such a cruel master as Satan, and there was never a bondage as awful as the bondage of sin.

Every person who is not in Christ is a slave. But when you come to Jesus Christ He sets you free. "If you continue in my word, then are ye my disciples indeed; And ye shall know the truth, and the truth shall make you free. . . .If the Son therefore shall make you free, ye shall be free indeed" (John 8:31-32,36). The Lord Jesus Christ takes every man and woman who believes in Him and sets them free from the power of every sin.

Christians are happy because they know that they are children of God. It is a wonderful thing to know that you are a child of God. No one knows it but the Christian, for only the Christian is a child of God.

How does the Christian know that he is a child of God? Because God says so. "As many as received him, to them gave he power to become the sons of God, even to them that believe on his name" (John 1:12).

The moment you accept the Lord Jesus Christ, you will be a child of God and know that you are a child of God. Isn't that enough to be happy about? Suppose you knew that you were the son of some great man or the son of a millionaire or the son of a king—don't you think you would be happy? But being the son of any king is nothing compared to being the son of God, the King of kings.

One day, many years ago, an English duke lay dying. He called his younger brother to his bedside and said, "Brother, in a few hours you will be a duke—and I will be a king." He was a Christian. He was a child of a King, and he knew that when he left this world, he would get a kingdom up there. The moment anyone receives Jesus Christ, even if he is the poorest man on earth, he can lift up his head and say, "I am a child of a King. I know I am a child of God."

Sometimes, as I travel around the world, people will point out a man to me and say, "That man is the son of a great man." What of it? Suppose he is a child of a king? I am a child of God. That is better than being a child of a king.

We read in the Bible that the gospel was preached to the poor. I believe in preaching to the rich. They need it as much as anybody. But I would rather be a poor man that is a child of God than a rich man that is a child of the devil.

Nothing To Fear

Christians are happy because they are delivered from all fear. A Christian who believes the Bible, studies it, and remembers it is not afraid of anything or anybody. A great many wealthy people have all their joy spoiled because they are constantly thinking that some calamity may overtake them. People who have all the comforts of life don't enjoy them because they fear that some calamity may come and sweep the comforts away. Those with very little, who are perhaps just making a living, don't enjoy it because they fear they may be thrown out of work and not be able to make a living. The true Christian is delivered from all those fears.

There is one verse in the Bible which will take away all anxiety as long as you live. "And we know that all things work together for good to them that love God" (Romans 8:28).

If a person believes the Bible and keeps it in mind, he is not afraid of calamity, neither is he afraid of any man. Many people are afraid of men and tormented by the fear of men. They would take a stand as a Christian, but they are afraid of being laughed at or persecuted at home or on their jobs. But a Christian is not afraid of man. The Christian reads Romans 8:31 and says, "If God be for us, who can be against us?" A Christian does not fear any man or woman on earth.

In Chicago a man came to me and said, "You had better look out. There is a man who says he has it in for you." He told me who the man was—a very desperate man, a man willing to do almost anything. I was not troubled a bit. I did not lie awake a single night. I was not worried for two seconds.

I said, "That is all right. I know he is quite powerful, and I have reason to believe he will do anything, but I know that I am right with God. God is on my side, and that man can't touch me." A living faith in Jesus Christ takes away all fear of man forever.

It takes away the fear of death. People's lives are shadowed and darkened by the fear of death. Right in the midst of health and strength they say, "Oh, what if I have some terrible disease!" But death has lost all its terror for the Christian. A Christian knows that what men call death is for him simply to depart and be with Christ.

There is one word that fills the heart of the Christian with joy, but fills the heart of the unsaved with terror. That word is *eternity*. In eternity, sorrow, separation, sickness, and death are over forever. All is eternal sunshine. A Christian is delivered from fear of eternity. To people who do not know Christ, eternity is a dreadful thing to think about. But for people in Christ, eternity is the sweetest thing there is to think about.

Write out a card with these words, "Where will you spend eternity?" If you hand it to a man who is not a Christian, it will make him mad. But hand it to a Christian, and he will rejoice. He will answer, "Why, I will spend eternity with Christ in glory!"

The Joy Of Everlasting Life

Christians are happy because they know they will live forever. It is a wonderful thing to know that you will never die, that throughout the endless ages you will live on and on. "And the world passeth away, and the lust thereof: but he that doeth the will of God abideth for ever" (1 John 2:17). "He that believeth on the Son hath everlasting life: and he that believeth not the Son shall not see life; but the wrath of God abideth on him" (John 3:36).

Before I was a Christian I did not like to look into the future, but how I love to look into the future now! It is a great joy to preach, but oh, to be able to stand and look down through the coming ages and see them roll on, age after age, and know that you are going to live for all eternity in happiness and joy ever increasing! I am not surprised that Christians are happy. I don't wonder that they have "joy unspeakable and full of glory."

Christians know that they are heirs of God and joint-heirs with Jesus Christ. They know that they have an inheritance incorruptible, undefiled, and that does not fade away, laid up in store in heaven for them. When someone rides down beautiful country roads and looks out at the beautiful mansions and sees the lakes, forests, parks, and the gardens, he may say, "It must be very pleasant to live there." I suppose it is, but how long will those people live there? They will soon be gone.

But every man, woman, and child who takes Jesus will have an inheritance that will last forever. Every earthly inheritance soon fails—even the richest man on earth won't keep his property very long. But the poorest man who will take Jesus Christ will get an inheritance that will last forever.

One day a poor English girl was traveling by train and looking out of the window. They passed by beautiful farms and mansions. Every once in a while the poor girl said with a smile, "That belongs to my Father." They would come to a farm and she would say, "That belongs to my Father;" then to a beautiful mansion, "That belongs to my Father, too;" then they would pass a castle, and she would say, "That belongs to my Father."

Finally, the man who was listening turned to her and said, "Well, miss, you must have a rich Father."

She said, "He is—I am a child of God." She was very rich.

You may be having a hard time in this world. You may have to work long hours for small pay. Perhaps your home is not very comfortable. Well, you won't have to live here very long. If you receive Christ, you are going to a mansion like this earth never saw and to such an inheritance as no man ever inherited on this earth. If you will take Jesus Christ, you will know that you are an heir to all God has. The whole world belongs to Him— the cattle on a thousand hills. (See Psalm 50:10.)

If you are a child of God, if you will take Christ, you will be heir to all He is and all He has.

The Holy Spirit Living Within

Christians are happy because God gives them the Holy Spirit to dwell in their hearts. When the Holy Spirit dwells in the heart, He fills the heart with sunshine and gladness and joy unspeakable.

One Monday morning a woman came to my door, rang the bell, and said she wanted to see me. My daughter said, "You know he sees no one on Monday." She said, "I know it, but I have got to see him." When I came down, I saw one of the members of my church—a poor woman who had to work hard for her living.

"Oh," she said, "Mr. Torrey, I knew you didn't see anybody on Monday, and I didn't like to trouble you, but I received the Holy Spirit last night. I could not sleep all night, and I made up my mind that I was going to give up one day's work, and just come and tell you how happy I was. I just had to. I can't very well afford to give up a day's work, but my heart is so full of joy I could not keep still. I had to tell somebody, and I didn't know anybody else I wanted to tell as much as I wanted to tell you. Though I knew you didn't see anybody on Monday, I thought you would be glad to have me come and tell you."

"Yes," I said, "I am glad." That woman was so happy that she could not work; her heart was full of joy.

I don't care how discouraged your heart is today or how full of sadness you are. I don't care if you think your situation is hopeless. If you will take Jesus Christ as your Savior and surrender your whole heart and your whole life to Him, your heart will be filled with a sweetness above anything to be known this side of heaven.

A Christian can rejoice with joy unspeakable and full of glory. But you have to be a true Christian. Just going to church won't do it; just saying your prayers won't do; just reading the Bible or a prayer book won't do; just being baptized and confirmed won't do it; just going to the Lord's Supper won't do. But if you take Jesus into your heart to be your Savior to rule and reign there and surrender all to Him, you will get a joy that is heaven on earth.

People say to me, "Do you expect to go to heaven?" Yes, I know I am going to heaven; but, thank God, I am in heaven now. I have now a present heaven to live in until I go to the future heaven.

I feel like singing all the time. I used to be one of the most depressed men on earth. I was despondent; I was gloomy; I used to sit and have the blues by the hour. But I never have had the blues since I accepted the Lord Jesus. I have had trouble. I have had trials. I have seen the time when I had a wife and four children and not a penny to buy them another meal. But it came in time, for I knew where to go—right to God, and He provided. I knew Whom I trusted. I knew He would get me out somehow, and He did.

If you want darkness turned into sunshine, if you want sadness turned into joy, if you want despair turned into glory, if you want defeat turned into victory, if you want all that is bad turned into all that is good—receive the Lord Jesus Christ, and receive Him right now.

Chapter 14

THE FEAR OF MAN

"The fear of man bringeth a snare: but whoso putteth his trust in the Lord shall be safe"—Proverbs 29:25.

Two paths lay open before us—one of ruin, the other of salvation. The fear of man brings a snare—ruin—but whoever puts his trust in the Lord shall be safe. The way of salvation is trust in Jehovah. Even if you do not believe another verse in the Bible, you know that verse is true. I don't care how much of an unbeliever a man may be, he knows that the fear of what others will think brings a snare.

Once a young fellow came to Chicago who was too much of a man to gamble. But he liked an occasional innocent game of cards. One night he was playing cards with his friends, and someone suggested that they put up a dollar to make it interesting. "Oh," they said, "we don't care for the money, but it is just to lend interest to the game."

"No," he said. "I never gamble. I think gambling is stealing." He is right, for gambling is stealing. No self-respecting man wants another man's money. I don't see how a man who has taken another man's money by gambling can look in the mirror.

He insisted, "No. Gambling is rank dishonesty; I never gamble."

"Oh," they said, "it is not gambling; it is just for a little amusement. You better go home and go to Sunday school. Go and sit with your mother." They ridiculed him into his first game of cards for money. The gambler's passion—a harder passion to overcome then the appetite for drink ever was—seized him. He ended up behind prison bars because he gambled until he took his employer's money to gamble with. The fear of man brought a snare that landed him in prison.

Afraid To Take A Stand

The fear of man ensnares Christians into a denial of their Lord. It did Peter. He told his Lord that though all forsake Him, he never would. But when the servant girl accused him of being a follower of Jesus of Nazareth, he said, "I don't know the man." A few moments later he repeated his denial, and an hour after, with oaths and cursings, frightened by what a servant girl may do or say, he denied his Lord. (See Matthew 26:69-75.)

Many of you are doing the same every day. In your office or shop or factory, Jesus Christ is ridiculed. Hard things are said about the Bible; the name of the Lord that died upon the cross of Calvary for you is taken in blasphemy, and you are not man enough or woman enough to stand up and say, "I am a Christian. I believe in that Christ whom you are ridiculing. I believe in that Bible you are laughing at." You are afraid to be laughed at, and the fear of man has ensnared you into a denial of the Lord who died on the cross for you.

The fear of man ensnares professed Christians into a guilty compromise with the world. Are you doing things in family life, social life, and business life that you know are wrong? Your best moral judgment condemns you every time you do them, but you say, "Well, everybody does them. I will be considered odd if I don't do them."

A Christian man living in one of the suburbs of Chicago said to me, "My daughter is practically ostracized because she won't drink." Thank God, she was woman enough, though she was still a young girl, to be willing to be ostracized rather than compromise. Many people are not.

Would you rather not participate in worldly entertainment? You know you don't feel happy or comfortable there. But you are not brave enough to stand for modesty, purity, and God. The fear of man has entangled you in a snare which has robbed you by your compromise of every bit of real power for Jesus Christ.

150

Slothful Silence

The fear of man ensnares Christians into a guilty silence and inactivity. When the invitation is given out for Christians to go to work and speak to the unsaved, few want to do it. Oh, you would like to lead someone to Christ. What a joy it would be to you. But you say, "Suppose I talk to somebody and they don't like it; suppose they laugh at me; suppose they say some hard things to me." The fear of man in your home, in your shop, in your hotel, everywhere you go, is shutting your mouth and robbing you of the joy of leading others to Jesus Christ.

Well, suppose they do laugh at you. They spat in your Master's face. They won't spit in yours. They struck Him with their fists. They probably won't strike you. They nailed Him to the cross. Are you not willing to be laughed at for a Master like that?

I believe that the fear of man which keeps Christians back from giving their testimony for Christ and working to bring others to Christ does far more to hinder the work of God than any other cause. Men are being saved by the thousands, but if Christians would abandon their fear and have the boldness to witness and work for their Master, people would be saved by the tens of thousands.

The fear of man ensnares those who are not Christians into the rejection of Jesus Christ. There are hundreds of men and women who would like to be Christians. They see the joy of it.

But they are afraid that if they accept Christ somebody will ridicule them. The fear of man shuts them out of the acceptance of Jesus Christ. I believe that more people are kept from accepting Christ by the fear of what someone will say or do than by any other cause. If we could get rid of this fear, there would be thousands saved every night at evangelistic crusades instead of two or three hundred.

The fear of man ensnares those who think they have accepted Christ into not making a public confession of Christ. Jesus says distinctly, "Whosoever therefore shall confess me before men, him will I also confess before my Father which is in heaven. But whosoever shall deny me before men, him will I also deny before my Father which is in heaven" (Matthew 10:32-33).

Paul says distinctly, "With the heart man believeth unto righteousness, and with the mouth confession is made unto salvation" (Romans 10:10). Yet, a host of men and women are trying to be Christians and never stand up to say so. "I don't believe in this publicity. I don't believe in this standing-up business. I believe in doing things more quietly. I don't believe in excitement." You can give a thousand and one reasons, but if you were honest with yourself, as you will have to be honest with God some day, you would say, "It is because I am afraid to do it."

A fine looking young fellow came to me one day and said, "I am a fool."

I said, "What is the matter?"

He said, "I thought I accepted Christ here the other night, and I have not been man enough to tell another man in the office what I have done. I am a fool."

Well, he was. So are you. You professed to receive Jesus Christ, but to this day you have not told the other men in your office, in your home, in your hotel, in your shop. The fear of man has sealed your mouth, made you a coward, and robbed you of all the joy that there is in a bold Christian experience.

The fear of man ensnares those who start out in the Christian life from going on in it, because somebody says something discouraging. One night two young men both professed to accept Christ at a crusade meeting. One of the men went to his pastor and told him what he had done. His pastor encouraged him in his new walk with Christ.

The other man's pastor was one of those convivial pastors, a man whose chief function is to serve as a figurehead at large banquets where he joins in and encourages the drinking and frivolity. The young convert went to this preacher and told him what he had done. His preacher said, "Don't you believe a word they are saying up there." He discouraged him. There must be a deep spot in hell for the man that bears the name of minister and dares to discourage a young convert in his first aspirations toward God.

The poor young fellow was discouraged entirely. A minister of the gospel had laughed at him and snared him into wretched backsliding and maybe even into hell. If you are starting out in the Christian life, no matter who approves or disapproves, you are on the right track. Go on in spite of everybody.

Eternal Consequences

The fear of man ensnares people to their eternal ruin. Many men and women lie in Christless graves and will spend a Christless eternity because the fear of man kept them from the acceptance of Christ. One night after speaking, I gave the altar call. Among those who were moved by the Spirit of God was a young woman. She rose to her feet and started to come to the front. The young man who sat beside her touched her arm. He was engaged to marry her. He said, "Don't go tonight. If you will wait for a few days I may go with you." For fear of offending her fiance, she sat down.

I went back the next week to speak at the same place. At the close of the meeting two young women came and said, "Oh, Mr. Torrey, just as soon as you can get away from the meeting here, come with us. There is a young lady who was going to come forward the other night, but the young man to whom she is engaged asked her to wait. She did wait, and now she has scarlet fever. She probably won't live until morning. Come to see her just as soon as you can get away from the meeting."

I left as soon as I could. I entered her home and went into the room where the poor girl lay dying, hardly recognizable as the same person, but perfectly conscious. I urged her to accept Christ. "No," she said, "I was about to receive Him the last time you were here. I didn't repent then. I am dying; I can't repent now."

I begged her. I knew it was her last hour. I did everything, but she would not yield. When I left that room of awful darkness, a young man in the hallway grasped me by the hand. He was shaking like a leaf. "Oh," he said, "Mr. Torrey, I am engaged to marry that girl. Now she is dying without Christ. She is lost, and I am to blame. I am to blame."

The Spirit of God is moving on this earth with mighty power. Many of you are on the verge of a decision for Christ. Don't let the fear of man frighten you out of taking your stand now.

Trusting The Lord

Our text in Proverbs 29:25 promises, "Whoso putteth his trust in the Lord shall be safe." He will be safe from all danger of yielding to sin and temptation. If you trust God, temptation has no power over you. A man cannot yield to temptation without distrusting God.

Every act of sin is an act of distrust of God. He

that trusts God will do right though the heavens fall.

I knew a businessman who lost nearly everything he owned and had to sell everything in order to pay his debts. He paid all his debts, but it left him practically penniless. Then he was offered a job with a manufacturing firm. He came to me and said, "What shall I do? This is an excellent company to work for. They said they will promote me quickly, but if I take this post, I must work on Sundays. What shall I do?"

I said, "Well, you will have to decide for yourself, but if you can't do it with a clear conscience, you can't afford to do it."

He said, "I can't do it with a clear conscience." He refused the position, although he did not know what he was to do to support himself and his wife and family of three children. A day or two later, he got a job at very low wages. A few weeks after that he got a position at several hundred dollars per month. He went on to become the controller of one of the biggest mercantile establishments in the Northwest—all because he trusted God.

When I was home this summer, I found that a young Jewish woman had been converted while I was away. She was a very talented woman, but she had to work hard for her living to support the family. After she was converted, she was full of love for Christ. She went out to the place where she worked, a very large company, and she began talking about Christ to the other employees.

Some of them did not like it. They went to the head of the firm and said, "She is constantly talking to us about Christ. We don't like it."

The managers called her in and said, "We have no objection to Christianity, no objection to you being a Christian. It is a good thing, but you must not talk about it at this company."

"Very well," she said. "I won't work where I can't take Christ with me and talk for my Master."

"Well, then," they said, "you will have to lose your job."

"Very well," she said, "I will give up my position before I will be disloyal to Jesus Christ."

They said, "Go back to work, and we will tell you our decision later." She went back to work.

At the end of the week, she got a letter from the firm. She said, "Here is my discharge," and she tore it open. The letter read, "We have a position with great responsibility, with a much larger salary than you are getting. We think you are the woman for the position, and we offer it to you." They saw she could be trusted. Businessmen are looking for men and women whom they can trust.

Facing Persecution

Whoever trusts in the Lord will be safe from danger of every kind. We read in Romans 8:31, "If God be for us, who can be against us?" Men will persecute you. They will ridicule you. They will do all they can to harm you. Jesus said in John

157

15:20, "If they have persecuted me, they will also persecute you." But it won't do you any harm.

Some people are frightened at the thought of being persecuted. But it is one of the greatest privileges on earth for converts to be persecuted for Jesus Christ. "Blessed are ye, when men shall revile you, and persecute you, and shall say all manner of evil against you falsely, for my sake. Rejoice, and be exceeding glad: for great is your reward in heaven" (Matthew 5:11-12).

When we were in Australia an organized gang came to break up our meeting. I had said some rather plain things about living a holy life before God that angered a number of people. This gang which came to break up the meetings was seated in the far gallery. The power of God came down, and two ringleaders walked right up from that gallery the whole length of the hall and came down to the front. They turned and faced the crowd and said, "We accept Jesus Christ."

The next day some friends of the ringleader of the gang met him on the street. They knocked him down and pounded him to make him swear and curse God. But God had taken all the swearing out of him. Instead of swearing, he wrote one of the most beautiful letters to a friend of his, who sent it to me. He wrote about the joy of suffering for Jesus' sake.

They may persecute you. They may pound you, they may hound you, but they can't hurt you if you are right with God. The man who trusts in the Lord is eternally safe.

Jesus says in John 10:28-29, "I give unto them eternal life; and they shall never perish, neither shall any man pluck them out of my hand. My Father, which gave them me, is greater than all; and no man is able to pluck them out of my Father's hand." If you trust in the Lord, God the Father Almighty's hand is underneath you and around you; Christ the Son's hand is over you and around about you. You are in between the almighty hand of God the Father and God the Son, and all the devils in hell can't get you.

Throw away your fear of man. In place of it put trust in Jehovah. You compromising Christians, throw away your compromise. Be radical for Jesus, be a clean, straight Christian for God. Throw away your guilty silence. Go to work to bring others to Christ, and keep it up tomorrow, the next day, and the day after that. Throw away your guilty silence about unpopular truth, and declare the whole counsel of God, even though they say you are old fashioned because you tell the truth. Don't worry about what anybody says, but stand up boldly and confess Christ before the world.

The Time For Harvest

In the early days of Mr. Moody's work in Chicago, there was a man who regularly attended the church. He seemed to be on the point of decision for Christ. At last Mr. Moody went to him and urged him to decide at once. He replied that he could not take a stand for Christ. There was a man with whom he worked who would ridicule him, and he could not endure his ridicule. As Mr. Moody kept urging him to make a decision, the man at last became irritated and ceased attending the church.

Some months after, when the man had quite dropped out of sight, Mr. Moody received an urgent call to go and see the man at once. He found him very ill, apparently dying, and in great anxiety about his soul. Mr. Moody showed him the way of life, and the man professed to accept Christ. His soul seemed at rest. To everyone's surprise, he took a turn for the better, and full recovery seemed sure.

Mr. Moody called upon him one day and found him sitting out in the sunshine. Mr. Moody said, "Now that you have accepted Christ, and God has raised you up, you must come and confess Him publicly as soon as you are able to come to church."

To Mr. Moody's astonishment the man replied, "No, not now. I don't dare admit I am a Christian in Chicago. But I intend to move to Michigan soon. As soon as I get over there, I will come out publicly and take my stand for Christ." Mr. Moody told him that Christ could protect him in Chicago as well as in Michigan, but the man's fear of his friend held him back. Mr. Moody was greatly disappointed and left.

One week from that day, the man's wife called Mr. Moody and begged him to come at once and see her husband. He had suffered a relapse, was worse than ever, and a council of physicians agreed that there was no possibility of recovery.

"Did he send for me to come?" asked Mr. Moody.

"No. He says that he is lost, and that there is no hope for him. He does not wish to see you or speak to you, but I cannot let him die this way. You must come."

Mr. Moody hastened to the house and found the man in a state of utter despair. To all Mr. Moody's pleas for him to take Christ, he would reply that it was too late, that he was lost, that he had thrown away his day of opportunity, and that he could not be saved now. Mr. Moody said, "I will pray for you."

"No," said the man, "don't pray for me. It is useless. I am lost. Pray for my wife and children. They need your prayers."

Mr. Moody knelt down by his side and prayed, but his prayers did not seem to go higher than his head. He could not get hold of God for this man's salvation. When he arose the man said, "There, Mr. Moody, I knew that prayer would do no good. I am lost."

With a heavy heart Mr. Moody left the house. All afternoon the man kept repeating, "The harvest is past, the summer is ended, and I am not saved." (See Jeremiah 8:20.) Just as the sun was setting

161

behind the western prairies, the man passed away. In his last moment they heard him murmuring, "The harvest is past, the summer is ended, and I am not saved." Another soul went out into eternity unprepared, snared into eternal perdition by the fear of man. Throw away your fear of man and put your trust in the Lord and be saved.

Chapter 15

HOW GOD LOVED THE WORLD

"For God so loved the world, that he gave his only begotten Son, that whosoever believeth in him should not perish, but have everlasting life"—John 3:16.

Thousands of people have been saved by that wonderful verse; tens of thousands, hundreds of thousands, by simply reading it in the Bible. That one verse tells us some very important things about the love of God. It tells us that our salvation begins in God's love. We are not saved because we love God; we are saved because God loves us. Our salvation begins in God's loving us, and it ends in our loving God.

The first thing our text teaches us about the love of God is that the love of God is universal. "God so loved *the world*"—not some part of it, not some elect people or some select class. God loves the rich, but God loves the poor, too. The rich need to hear the gospel just as much as the poor, and they are not nearly as likely to. If some poor man who did not even know where he was going to sleep tonight stood up to receive Christ, many people would not think it amounted to much. But God would be just as pleased to see the poorest man or woman accept Christ as He would be to see the richest millionaire. God loves the man who can't read or write as much as He loves the most brilliant scientist or philosopher that there is on earth.

If some university professor was converted, some people would be delighted. They would say, "Oh, a wonderful thing happened. One of our learned professors was converted." But if some man or woman that can't even read or write stood up to accept Christ, some people would not be nearly as impressed. The most wonderful thing of all about it is this—God loves the moral, the upright, the virtuous, the righteous, and God just as truly loves the sinner, the outcast, the abandoned, and the bad.

One night I was visiting one of the members of my church, and his little girl was playing around the room. The child did something naughty, and her father called out, "Don't be naughty. If you are a good girl, God will love you, but if you are not, God won't love you."

I said, "Charlie, what nonsense are you teaching that child of yours? That is not what my Bible teaches. My Bible teaches that God loves the sinner just as truly as He loves the saint."

It is hard to make people believe that God does

love the sinner and the outcast. This is the truth that the Bible emphasizes the most.

Christ Died For Sinners

I was preaching one hot summer's night, so hot that the windows were all taken out at the back to let a little fresh air in. The room was packed. At the back of the room a man was sitting on the windowsill. When I asked for all who wished to be saved that night to hold up their hands, that man raised his hand. But as soon as I pronounced the benediction, he started for the door. I forgot all about my after-meeting. All I saw was that man starting for the door, and I started after him. I caught him just as he turned to descend the stairway. I laid my hand upon his shoulder and said to him, "My friend, you held up your hand to say you wanted to be saved."

"Yes, I did."

"Why didn't you stay, then, to the second meeting?"

He said, "It is no use."

"Why?" I said. "God loves you."

He said, "You don't know who you are talking to. I am the worst thief in this town."

"Well," I said, "even if you are, I can prove to you from the Bible that God loves you." I opened my Bible to Romans 5:8, and I read, "God commendeth his love toward us, in that, while we were yet sinners, Christ died for us."

"Now," I said, "if you are the worst thief in

town, you are certainly a sinner, and that verse says that God loves sinners."

It broke the man's heart, and he began to weep. I took him to my office where we sat down, and he told me his story. He said, "I was released from prison this morning. I had started out this evening with some companions to commit one of the most daring burglaries that was ever committed in this city. By tomorrow morning I would either have had a big stake of money or a bullet in my body. But as we were going down the street together, we passed the corner where you were holding that open-air meeting. A Scotchman was speaking. My mother was Scotch, and when I heard that Scotch accent it reminded me of my mother.

"I had a dream about my mother the other night in prison. I dreamed that my mother came to me and begged me to give up my wicked life. When I heard that Scotchman talk I stopped to listen. My two pals said, 'Come along,' and cursed me. I said, 'I am going to listen to what this man says.' Then they tried to drag me across the street, but I would not go. What that man said touched my heart. When he invited everyone to this meeting, I came, and that is why I am here."

I opened my Bible, and I showed him that God loves sinners, that Christ had died for sinners, and that he could be saved by simply accepting Christ. He did accept Christ. We knelt down side by side, and that man offered the most wonderful prayer I ever heard in all my life.

Are you a thief? God loves you. Are you an unbeliever? God loves you. Are you a blasphemer? God loves you. You can't find in all the earth a man or woman that God doesn't love.

The Character Of God's Love

The second thing our text teaches us about the love of God is that God's love is a holy love. "God *so* loved the world, that he gave his only begotten Son." A great many people cannot understand that. They say, "I cannot see why it is if God loves me that He doesn't forgive my sins outright without His Son dying in my place. I cannot see the necessity of Christ's death. If God is love, and if God loves me and everybody else, why doesn't He take us to heaven right away without Christ dying for us?"

The text answers the question, "God *so* loved." That "so" brings out the character of God's love. God could not and would not pardon sin without an atonement. God is a holy God. God's holiness must manifest itself in some way. It must either manifest itself in the punishment of the sinner—that is, in our eternal banishment from His presence—or it must manifest itself in some other way.

The death of Jesus Christ upon the cross of Calvary was God providing atonement for sinful man. But some men say, "That is not fair. Are you saying that God took the sin of man and laid it upon Jesus Christ, an innocent third Person? That is not fair."

But Jesus Christ was not a third Person. "God was in Christ reconciling the world unto himself" (2 Corinthians 5:19). The atoning death of Jesus Christ on the cross is not God taking my sin from me and laying it on a third person. It is God the Father taking the penalty of my sin into His own heart and dying in His Son, in my place. Jesus Christ was not merely the first Person. He was the second Person, too. Jesus Christ was the Son of Man, the second Adam, the representative man. No ordinary man could have died for you and me. It would have been of no value. But Jesus Christ was the second Adam, your representative and mine. When Christ died on the cross of Calvary, I died in Him, and the penalty of my sin was paid.

If you do not believe in the deity of Christ, the atonement becomes irrational. If you remove the humanity of Christ and believe He is merely divine, the atonement becomes irrational. But take all that the Bible says—that God was in Christ, and that in Christ the Word became God manifest in the flesh—and the atonement of Christ is the most profound and wonderful truth the world has ever seen.

God's love was a holy love. In His perfect righteousness, perfect justice, perfect holiness, as well as perfect love through Christ's atoning death, He could pardon and save the vilest of sinners. When you are awakened to a proper sense of your sinfulness, when you see yourself as you really are, and when you see God as He really is, nothing will satisfy your conscience but the doctrine that God, the Holy One, substituted His atoning action for His punitive action. In the death of Jesus Christ on the cross of Calvary your sin and mine was perfectly settled forever.

Thank God, the law of God has no claim upon me. I broke it, I admit it, but Jesus Christ kept it. He satisfied its punitive claim by dying for those who had not kept it. On the ground of that atoning death there is pardon for the vilest sinner.

You may have gone deeper into sin than you realize yourself, but while your sins are as high as the mountains, the atonement that covers them is as high as heaven. While your sins are as deep as the ocean, the atonement that swallows them up is as deep as eternity. On the ground of Christ's atoning death there is pardon for the vilest sinner on earth.

God's Infinite Love

The third thing our text teaches us about the love of God is the greatness of that love. We see His love in the greatness of the gift He offers us—eternal life. It means a life that is perfect and divine in its quality as well as endless in its duration. "God so loved the world, that he gave his only begotten Son, that whosoever believeth in him should not perish but have *everlasting life.*"

I thank God for a life that is perfect in quality and that will never end. Most of us will have to die before long, as far as our physical life is concerned. Eighty years from now, you and most of your family and friends will be gone, unless the Lord comes back first. You may say that eighty years is a long time. No, it is not. It sounds long to young people; but when you get to be older, it looks very short. When the eighty years are up, what then? Suppose I had a guarantee that I was going to live two hundred years in perfect health, strength, and prosperity. Would that satisfy me? No, it would not. For when the two hundred years are up, what then? I want something that never ends, and thank God, in Christ I have something that never ends—eternal life! Who can have it? Anybody. "Whosoever believeth on Him."

Somebody asked a little boy, "What does whosoever mean?" The little fellow answered, "It means you and me and everybody else." When I read that "God so loved the world, that he gave his only begotten Son, that *whosoever* believeth on him," I know that means me. Thank God it did, and it means everybody else.

The Measure Of Love

The text tells us a second way in which the greatness of the love of God shows itself—in the sacrifice that God made for us. "God so loved the world, that he gave his only begotten Son." The measure of love is sacrifice. You can tell how much anybody loves you by the sacrifice that he is willing to make for you. God has shown the measure of His love by the sacrifice He made. He gave His very best, the dearest that He had.

No earthly father ever loved his son as God loved Jesus Christ. I have an only son; how I love him! But suppose some day I should see that boy of mine arrested by the enemies of Christ; and suppose they blindfolded him, spat in his face, beat him, and then made a crown of big, cruel thorns and put it on his brow, causing the blood to pour down his face on either side. How do you suppose I would feel?

Then suppose they stripped his garments from him, tied him to a post, and beat him with a stick that had long lashes of leather twisted with bits of brass and lead until his back was all torn and bleeding. How do you think I would feel?

Suppose they threw him down on a cross laid on the ground, stretched his right hand out on the arm of the cross, put a nail in the hand, lifted the heavy hammer and drove the nail through the hand; then they stretched his left arm on the other arm of the cross, put a nail in the palm of that hand, lifted the heavy hammer and sent the nail through that hand; then they drove the nail through his feet. Finally, they took that cross and plunged it into a hole and left him hanging there while the agony grew worse every minute. Suppose they left him to die beneath the burning sun. How do you suppose I would feel if I stood and looked on as my only boy dies in awful agony on a cross?

That is just what God saw. He loved His only begotten Son, as you and I never imagined loving our sons. He saw His Son hanging there, aching, all His bones out of joint, tortured in every part of His body! God looked on. Why did He permit it? Because He loved you and me, and it was the only way that we could be saved.

Your Response To God's Love

How are you going to repay that love? Some people will repay it with hatred. They hate God. They have never said it, but it is true.

A friend of mine was preaching one time in Connecticut. He was staying with a physician who had a beautiful, amiable daughter. She had never made a profession of faith, but she was such a beautiful person that people thought she was a Christian. One night, after the meetings had been going on for some time, my friend said to this young lady, "Are you going up to the meeting tonight?"

She said, "No, I am not."

He said, "I think you had better go."

"I will not go."

"Why," he said, "don't you love God?"

She said, "I hate God." She had never realized it before. I think she would have said she loved God up to that time, but when the demands of God were pressed home by the Holy Spirit, she was not willing to obey. She found out that she hated God.

Some of you have never found out that you hate God, but it is true. How have you used the name of

God today? You used it many times. In prayer? No, in profanity. Why? Because you hate God.

If a woman receives Christ, she may find that her husband will make life unbearable. Why? Because he hates God, and he wants to make his wife miserable for accepting His Son. If someone in your shop or your factory should accept Christ, you would laugh at them for it. Why? Because you hate God. Some people will read every heretical book they can get and go to every ungodly lecture. They are trying to convince themselves that the Bible is not God's Word. If anybody comes along and brings up some smart objection to the Bible, they laugh at it and rejoice in it. Why? Because they hate God and want to get rid of God's Book.

Some men and women love to hold up their heads and say, "I don't believe in the divinity of Christ. I don't believe He is the Son of God." Why? Because they hate God, and if they can rob His divine Son of the honor that belongs to Him, they will do it. They are repaying the wondrous love of God with hate.

Perhaps you refuse to accept Christ. You heard God's message of salvation many times. When people speak to you about committing your life to the Lord, you get angry. You say, "I wish you would not talk to me. It is none of your business whether I am a Christian or not." Why do you respond like this? Because you hate God.

Some people so bitterly hate God that they try to find fault with the doctrine of the atonement. They try to make themselves believe that Christ did not die on the cross for their salvation. They say, "I cannot understand the philosophy of it." A person who loved God would not stop to ask the philosophy of it. He would lift his heart in simple gratitude and praise to God for His great love and mercy.

Conquered By Love

There is one other thing that our text teaches us about the love of God—the conquering power of God's love. The love of God conquers sin, death, and wrong, and gives everlasting life. The love of God conquers where everything else fails.

The first time I ever preached in Chicago, I noticed a young woman who did not come forward when the rest came. I went down to where she was standing and urged her to come forward. She laughed and said, "No, I am not going forward," and sat down again.

The next night was not an evangelistic service, but a convention meeting. I was president of the convention. As I looked over the audience, I saw that young woman sitting in the back. She was elegantly dressed. I called somebody else to the platform and slipped around to the back part of the building. When the meeting was dismissed, I made my way to where that young lady was sitting. I sat down beside her and I said, "Won't you accept Christ tonight?"

"No," she said. "Would you like to know the

kind of life I am living?'' She was living in the best society, honored and respected. Then she told me a sad story of immorality and laughed as if it was a good joke.

I simply took my Bible and opened it to John 3:16. I passed it over to her and said, ''Won't you please read that?'' She had to hold it very near her eyes to see the small print, and she began in a laughing way. ''God so loved''—her laughter subsided—''the world''—there was nothing like a laugh now—''that he gave his only begotten Son.'' She burst into tears, and the tears flowed down on the elegant silk dress she was wearing. Hardened and shameless as she was, trifling as she was, one glimpse of Jesus on the cross of Calvary for her had broken her heart.

One night I was preaching, and we had an after-meeting. The leading soprano in the choir was not a Christian. She was a respectable girl, but very worldly and frivolous.

She decided to stay for the after-meeting. Her mother stood up in the congregation and said, ''I wish you would all pray for the conversion of my daughter.'' I did not turn to look at the choir, but I knew perfectly well how that young woman looked. I knew her cheeks were burning, I knew her eyes were flashing, and I knew that she was angry from the crown of her head to the soles of her feet.

As soon as the meeting was over, I hurried down to the door. As she came along, I walked toward her, held out my hand, and said, "Good evening, Cora." Her eyes flashed and her cheeks burned. She did not take my hand. She stamped her foot and said, "Mr. Torrey, my mother knows better than to do what she has done tonight. She knows it will only make me worse."

I said, "Cora, sit down." The angry girl sat down, and I opened my Bible at Isaiah 53:5 and handed it to her. I said, "Won't you please read it?" She read, "He was wounded for our transgressions, he was bruised for our iniquities: the chastisement of our peace was laid upon him." She did not get any further; she burst into tears. The love of God revealed in the cross of Christ had broken her heart, and she received Christ into her life.

Let the love of God conquer your stubborn, wicked, foolish, sinful, worldly, careless heart. "God so loved the world that he gave his only begotten Son that whosoever believeth in Him should not perish, but have everlasting life."

Yield to that love now.

Chapter 16

TODAY AND TOMORROW

"The Holy Ghost saith, To day"—Hebrews 3:7.
"Boast not thyself of tomorrow"—Proverbs
27:1.

Today is the wise man's day; tomorrow is the
fool's day. The wise man sees what ought to be
done and does it today. The foolish man says, "I
will do it tomorrow."

The men who always do the thing that should be
done today are successful for time and for eternity.
The men who put off until tomorrow what should
be done today will fail for time and eternity. "The
Holy Ghost saith, To day." Man, in the folly of his
heart, says, "Tomorrow."

I have no doubt that thousands of men and
women intend to be Christians at some time, but
they keep saying, "Not yet, not today." I am going
to tell you not merely why you should become a
Christian, but why you should become a Christian
today.

The sooner you come to Christ, the sooner you

will find the wonderful joy which is found in Him. In Jesus there is an immeasurably better joy than there is in the world—a purer joy, a higher joy, a holier joy, a more satisfying joy in every way.

This fact is not open to dispute. Everyone knows that it is true. Go to any person who has ever tried the world, and then tried Christ, and ask him, "Which joy is better—the joy which you found in the world or the joy which you have found in Christ?" You will get the same answer every time. The joy found in the world cannot for a moment be compared with the joy that is found in Christ.

If ever a person had an opportunity to try what this world can give, I had it, and I tried it. I tried all that could be found in the world, then I turned to Christ and tried Him. My testimony is just like the testimony of millions of others who have found that the joy of the world is nothing and the joy in Christ is everything. Any man who has really found Christ will tell you there is a joy in Christ higher, deeper, broader, wider, more wonderful in every way, than the joy that the world gives. The sooner you come to Christ, the sooner you will have that joy.

Deep And Abiding Peace

The sooner you come to Christ, the sooner you will escape the wretchedness and misery that there is away from Christ. First of all, there is the misery of an accusing conscience. No one out of Christ has peace of mind.

One night I was preaching to an audience of men and women to whom a twenty dollar bill would have been a great help. As I was preaching, I took out the money and held it up and said, "Now, is there a man in this audience who does not know Christ who has peace in his heart, deep abiding satisfaction and rest? If he will come up here and say so, I will give him this twenty dollar bill."

Nobody came up. When the meeting was over, I went down and stood at the door with the twenty dollar bill, for I thought they might be timid about coming up in front for it. I said, "If anybody can claim this twenty dollars by saying, 'I have peace of conscience and heart. My heart is satisfied without Christ,' he can have this twenty dollar bill." They filed out and nobody claimed the money. Finally, a man came along, and I said, "Don't you want this money?" He answered, "I cannot claim it on those conditions." Neither can you.

Another night I was preaching in Chicago, and I asked everybody in the building who had found rest and perfect satisfaction through the acceptance of Christ to stand up. More than a thousand men and women rose to their feet. I asked them to sit down, and then I said, "If there is an unbeliever in this house that can say he has found rest, peace, and perfect satisfaction of heart will he please stand?" There were a lot of agnostics and skeptics there. One man got up in the gallery, and I said, "I see there is a gentleman up there. I am glad that he has the courage of his convictions. I would like to speak with him after the meeting."

He came to the after-meeting. I said, "You stood up in the meeting tonight to say that you had perfect rest and peace of heart without Christ, and that your soul was satisfied with your unbelief. Was that true?"

"Oh," he said, "Mr. Torrey, that will have to be qualified." I guess it will. There is no peace, says my God, for the wicked. (See Isaiah 48:22.)

There is slavery in sin. "Whosoever committeth sin is the servant of sin" (John 8:34). Away from Christ is apprehension of what may happen, fear of disaster, fear of what man may do, fear of what may lie beyond the grave. When you come to Christ, you get rid of the fear of man. You have no fear of misfortune, for you are able to say, "All things work together for good to them that love God" (Romans 8:28). You have no fear of death, for what men call death is simply to depart and be with Christ. The moment you accept Christ, you get rid of the accusations of conscience, the slavery of sin, all fear of disaster, and the dread of death.

Why not get rid of it all right now? Suppose you were on the seashore and saw in the distance a wreck of a ship and a man clinging to a piece of wood. Every once in a while the cold waters sweep over him. Suppose you go out in a lifeboat and say to him, "I have come to rescue you. Get into the lifeboat!" Would the man say, "No, I think I can hold on until morning. Come out again in the morning, and I will get into the boat and come ashore." You would say, "Man, are you mad? Will you stay out here tonight when you can come ashore now?"

Oh, men and women, out on the wreck of life—the cold waves break over you with all the wretchedness of an accusing conscience, the bondage of sin, the fear of death, and all the multiplied wretchedness of the soul away from God—why cling to the wreck another night? You can come ashore to safety and joy now, if you will climb right into the lifeboat.

Working For The Lord

The sooner you come to Christ, the more you can do for Christ. The moment a person is saved he wants to do something for the Master. If you are saved a year from now, you will go to work for Christ, but there will be one year gone that will never come back. You can never go back over this year. You are associated with friends that you can lead to Christ now who may be past your reach then.

Before I was converted, I had a friend who lived in the same building. If I had been a Christian, I could have led him to Christ. Three years later, after I had accepted Christ, we had gone our separate ways.

I went back to the university to study for my second degree. One day my father picked up *The*

New York Times and began to read about a young man who was out playing ball. The man in centerfield threw the ball in. This young man's back was toward centerfield, and he was struck at the base of the brain. He never regained consciousness. My father said, "Isn't that your old friend?" I took the paper and read it and said, "Yes, it is my old friend." He was called into eternity without a moment's warning, and my opportunity of bringing him to Christ was gone forever!

In the years that have come since, God has used me to lead others to Christ, and I have often thought of Frank. In spite of all those who are now coming to Christ, Frank has gone, and my opportunity of leading him to Christ is lost forever. If you postpone taking Christ for thirty days, people that you might have reached during those thirty days will have passed beyond your reach forever.

In my first pastorate, a woman a little over fifty years of age who had been a backslider recommitted her life to the Lord. She became the best worker in the community. But her two sons had grown up during the years that she was far from God. They had both married and passed beyond her reach. Although she has been used to bring many to Christ, she was never able to bring these two sons to Christ. Her day of opportunity for them was while she was living in the world. Fathers and mothers living far from God, if you are not saved tonight, you may be some other day. But your sons and daughters will very likely have passed beyond your reach forever. The sooner you come to Christ, the more people you can bring with you.

The sooner you come to Christ, the richer will be your eternity. We are saved by grace, but we are rewarded according to our works. Every day after a man is saved, he lays up treasures in heaven. Every day you live for Christ, you will be that much richer for all eternity.

Some people have an idea that a man can be saved on his deathbed and have just as abundant an entrance into the Kingdom of God as he could have if he had been saved forty years. Neither common sense nor the Bible support that notion. A man may be saved on his deathbed, but he is saved "so as by fire" (1 Corinthians 3:15). His works are all burned up, and he enters heaven penniless. The man that is saved forty years before he dies and serves Christ for forty years, makes his deposits for which he will be richer throughout all eternity. "Lay up for yourselves treasures in heaven" (Matthew 6:20).

If you come to Christ while you are still young, you can enter the Kingdom of God with much fuller hands. I thank God I was converted when I was young, but what would I give for those wasted years while I deliberately resisted the Spirit of God! But I can't call them back.

The Day Of Salvation

The sooner you come to Christ, the surer you

are to come to Christ. If you are not saved tonight you may be tomorrow night, but you may not. I believe there are scores of people who will be saved now or never. People think they can turn to Christ when they decide that they want to, but when the Spirit of God is moving on your heart, it is a solemn moment. To say yes, means life; to say no, means death. To say yes, means heaven; to say no, means hell.

Often a man will be near the Kingdom, and he will say, "I am so interested I will certainly be just as interested tomorrow." But the critical hour has come, and if you do not yield now, you will have no interest tomorrow.

I once received a message from a wealthy young fellow saying that he wished to see me that night at Mr. Moody's meeting. I went and met him at the close of the meeting. He was on the verge of a decision. As we stood talking on the sidewalk, a bell rang out a late hour. I said to myself, "He is so near a decision I can leave him safely until tomorrow morning." So I said, "Good-night, Will. I will be around to your room tomorrow morning at ten."

It was one of the most fatal mistakes I ever made. I was there at ten and he was there, but his convictions had all left him. He was hard as stone. His opportunity had come and gone. You may be very near a decision at this moment, on the very borders of the Kingdom, but if you say, "No," tomorrow will be forever too late. Who of us can tell who will be called out of the world into eternity in a moment?

You have a chance now. Don't throw it away. The sooner you accept Christ, the surer you will be to receive Him. Ask Him into your heart now. You can have the joy of salvation at this moment; why wait a week? You can be saved from a life of wretchedness at once; why bear it another hour? The sooner you come to Christ, the more you can do for Him, and the richer you will be throughout all eternity.

Come to Him today and begin to lay up treasures in the bank of heaven. The sooner you come to Christ, the surer it is that you will come. Come now.

"The Holy Ghost saith, To day if ye will hear his voice, Harden not your hearts" (Hebrews 3:7-8).

"Boast not thyself of tomorrow; for thou knowest not what a day may bring forth" (Proverbs 27:1).

"Behold, now is the accepted time; behold, now is the day of salvation" (2 Corinthians 6:2).